Ingenious

Pleasures

Recencies Series: Research and Recovery in Twentieth-Century American Poetics
Matthew Hofer, Series Editor

This series stands at the intersection of critical investigation, historical documentation, and the preservation of cultural heritage. The series exists to illuminate the innovative poetics achievements of the recent past that remain relevant to the present. In addition to publishing monographs and edited volumes, it is also a venue for previously unpublished manuscripts, expanded reprints, and collections of major essays, letters, and interviews.

Also available in the Recencies Series:

A Description of Acquaintance: The Letters of Laura Riding and Gertrude Stein, 1927–1930 edited by Jane Malcolm and Logan Esdale
All This Thinking: The Correspondence of Bernadette Mayer and Clark Coolidge edited by Stephanie Anderson and Kristen Tapson
"A Serpentine Gesture": John Ashbery's Poetry and Phenomenology by Elisabeth W. Joyce
Evaluations of US Poetry since 1950, Volume 1: Language, Form, and Music edited by Robert von Hallberg and Robert Faggen
Evaluations of US Poetry since 1950, Volume 2: Mind, Nation, and Power edited by Robert von Hallberg and Robert Faggen
Expanding Authorship: Transformations in American Poetry since 1950 by Peter Middleton
Circling the Canon, Volume II: The Selected Book Reviews of Marjorie Perloff, 1995–2017 by Marjorie Perloff
Circling the Canon, Volume I: The Selected Book Reviews of Marjorie Perloff, 1969–1994 by Marjorie Perloff
Modernist Poetry and the Limitations of Materialist Theory: The Importance of Constructivist Values by Charles Altieri
Momentous Inconclusions: The Life and Work of Larry Eigner edited by Jennifer Bartlett and George Hart

For additional titles in the Recencies Series, please visit unmpress.com.

An Anthology of

punk

Trash

and

Camp

in

Twentieth-Century Poetry

Ingenious Pleasures

Edited by *Drew Gardner*

UNIVERSITY OF NEW MEXICO PRESS ALBUQUERQUE

©2023 by the University of New Mexico Press
All rights reserved. Published 2023
Printed in the United States of America

ISBN 978-0-8263-6493-7 (paper)
ISBN 978-0-8263-6494-4 (electronic)
Library of Congress Cataloging-in-Publication
data is on file with the Library of Congress

Founded in 1889, the University of New Mexico
sits on the traditional homelands of the
Pueblo of Sandia. The original peoples of New
Mexico—Pueblo, Navajo, and Apache—since time
immemorial have deep connections to the land
and have made significant contributions to the
broader community statewide. We honor the land
itself and those who remain stewards of this land
throughout the generations and also acknowledge
our committed relationship to Indigenous peoples.
We gratefully recognize our history.

Cover Photographs courtesy of Wikimedia Commons
and Isaac Morris
Cover and interior design by Isaac Morris
Composed in Athelas, Arial, Baskerville, Bely,
Brokenscript, and Cooper Std.

> We assume that there is something anarchic in all of us, something dangerous and wonderful that demands response...
> —Robert Christgau

> ask the bean sandwich
> —Charles Olson

> Novelty is better than repetition.
> —T. S. Eliot

> Art is the divine joke, and any *Public*, and any *Artist*, can see a nice, easy simple joke, such as the sun.
> —Mina Loy

Contents

Acknowledgments
xiii

Introduction
1

Baroness Elsa von Freytag-Loringhoven
Kindly
20

A Dozen Cocktails—Please
21

Subjoyride
23

Gertrude Stein
Breakfast
26

Idem the Same: A Valentine to Sherwood Anderson
29

Francis Picabia
Chimney Sperm
34

Apollinaire
Monday rue Christine
36

Mina Loy
from *Songs to Joannes*
38

Crab-Angel
39

Williams Carlos Williams
The Hermaphroditic Telephones
42

Breakfast
43

Hey Red!
44

Edith Sitwell
Ass-Face
45

Richard Huelsenbeck
End of the World
46

Abraham Lincoln Gillespie
A Poem From Puzlit
48

Tristan Tzara
from *Dada Manifestos*
49

Metal Coughdrops
51

Bern Porter
"What's filling lake Michigan faster than waste? Algae."
52

Sun Ra
Nuclear War
53

Jackson Mac Low
Asymmetry 372
55

Asymmetry 497
56

2nd Light Poem: For Diane Wakoski—10 June 1962
57

40TH DANCE—GIVING FALSELY—22 March 1964
60

A Lack of Balance But Not Fatal
61

Taylor Mead
from On Amphetamine and in Europe
64

Kenneth Koch
Everyone Is Endymion
66

Gypsy Yo-yo
68

No Job at Sarah Lawrence
69

from When The Sun Tries To Go On
71

Frank O'Hara
Fantasy
74

Russell Atkins
WEEKEND MURDER
76

John Ashbery
Leaving the Atocha Station
78

Hannah Weiner
from Weeks
81

Contents   ix

Edward Dorn
The Cosmology of Finding Your Spot
88

On the Edge of the Badlands
91

Mesozoic Landscape
92

The Turk
93

Kenward Elmslie
Sin in the Hinterlands
94

Ron Dossier
96

Hand
97

Nytol
98

from *Cyberspace*
99

Peter Orlovsky
Lines of Feeling
100

Ted Berrigan
Ass-face
102

Rochelle Owens
Not Be Essence That Cannot Be
103

Belonged into Sheepshank
104

Zu Zu Midday I'm Narcotic
105

Tom Raworth
Wandergut
106

Sally to See You, Tacitus
107

At Maximum Zero
108

How Cold Is Most
109

Clark Coolidge
"HEY! YOU LOOK LIKE A GIRL"
110

Acid
112

Fed Drapes
113

Crisp Loss
114

Machinations Calcite
115

The Automatic Nerve at Razed Heights
116

Pumper Mouth
117

Gulp
118

Jim Brodey
Bum Trip
119

Anne Tardos
from *Ginkgo Knuckle Nubia*
120

from *Considerations*
122

Aram Saroyan
"oh oh oh oh oh oh oh oh oh"
125

Bernadette Mayer
On Barnard
126

François Villon Follows the Thin Lion
127

Thick
128

We've Solved the Problem
129

A Catskill Eagle
130

Steve McCaffery
from *Teachable Texts*
131

Bob Perelman
PICTURE
133

DON'T DRINK THE WATER, EAT THE FOOD, OR BREATHE THE AIR
134

MENTAL IMAGERY
135

UP MEMORY LANE
136

SCAPEGOAT
137

Kathy Acker
Hello, I'm Erica Jong
138

Bruce Andrews
A small bird
140

Eagles Ate My Estrogen
141

from *Divestiture-A*
143

Charles Bernstein
Soapy Water
146

Claire-in-the-Building
148

Mao Tse Tung Wore Khakis
151

Michael Gottlieb
Timing Is Everything
152

Julie Patton
word / A. just poem
154

Kevin Davies
—] Keep losing things
155

—**plot.** but the people she gives it to
156

—some middle-distance cairn that, when approached, becomes just another
157

From each according to the vituperative whiplash of each understanding
158

The thrill of being misquoted, of inserting miniature cars in the urethra
159

Stacy Doris
from *Artic Uncles (on Rollerblades) Advance*
160

Contributors
169

Credits
189

Acknowledgments

Many Thanks: Bruce Andrews, Franklin Bruno, Jordan Davis, Katie Degentesh, Nada Gordon, Michael Golston, Matthew Hofer, Paul Stephens.

Introduction

Ingenious Pleasures identifies and follows a line of writing that cuts through received taxonomies of movements, influences, and styles, charting a new path through Modernism to the present. Moving through the twentieth century, the anthology focuses on the unexpected, the anarchic, the demotic, the absurd, the irreverent, the coarse, the rude, and the deliriously playful. It marks an alternative strain of Modernism that stretches from one side of the century to the other.

This line consists of *trash-punk*: collage-driven poetry that embodies the sensibilities of punk, camp, and trash in different proportions and fuses them into a single style and/or method. Punk might be thought of as a phenomenon of the decades following World War II, but the term itself can be projected back to the beginning of the century and even earlier. Greil Marcus sets a precedent for this approach in *Lipstick Traces* by connecting the late-century punk impulse retrospectively to Situationism and Dadaism and finally all the way back to medieval heretics who were called the Brethren of the Free Spirit.

While generally presenting an affront to mainstream poetry culture, trash-punk is rooted in a rebellious pleasure principle, a kind of friendly anti-art.

Anti-art is typically understood as a generalized attack on art, but some instantiations of it demonstrate an impulse toward *rescue* rather than a motive of *destruction*. If anti-art tries to sweep something away, rescue art tries to save something. Trash-punk exemplifies the latter. Thus this anthology features rescue art with a trash-punk sensibility. While "trash" and "punk" strictly speaking may be thought of as period designations, *trash-punk* as I am using the term can be traced back to the beginning of the 20th century. It is a conservative art in the literal sense: it seeks to *conserve* the animating principle of the creative act and its connection to the living present rather than attempting to maintain obsolete conventional forms, attitudes, and assumptions.

The moment of trash-punk's arrival is Dadaism, after the age of mass media had taken hold. Beginning in Zurich around 1915, and taken up in other European capitals, Dada came out of the impossibility of maintaining any positive assumptions about authority, major institutions, or hierarchies of culture after the disaster of World War I. Poetry reflected what was going on, and art was reframed as "an opportunity for the true perception and criticism of the times we live in," as Hugo Ball put it. The advent of Dadaism also coincided with Einstein's publication of the Theory of General Relativity, his discovery that time and space are not absolute but are relative to observers' frames of reference—that they are not separate at all but are part of a single manifold. This moment—which at once undermined not only the accepted structure of power, authority, and respectability, but also the apparent structure of the fabric of reality itself—is where trash-punk begins.

Dadaism is this book's point of departure, but the later Modernist strain of poetry it charts has no manifestos, and its dynamics don't include the brittle stridency that tended to accompany early avant-garde movements. Techniques and concerns that overlap with Dada recur throughout this anthology, though: in the extensive use of collage, in the inclusion of materials typically considered debased or un-poetic, in the humor and a general attitude of performative absurdity and irrational, joyful wit. Dada's creative acts entailed an anarchic playfulness and a strong desacralizing tendency. These are qualities that also overlap with punk rock, camp, and trash sensibilities.

Trash-punk has persisted in the background for decades—many different poets have moved in and out of its magnetic field in different ways over time.

Bits and pieces and hints of the hidden Modernist line of trash-punk appear in older poetry. One finds it, for instance, in the setting aside of binaries and the drastic, slangy spontaneity of some Zen poetry, such as the eighteenth- to nineteenth-century poet Issa.

> The toad! It looks like
> it could belch
> a cloud

or

> Writing shit about new snow
> for the rich
> is not art

or this, from the Zenrin anthology:

> At Mount Wu-T'ai the clouds are steaming rice
> Before the ancient Budda Hall
> dogs piss at heaven

Along different lines, Catullus overlaps with trash-punk sensibilities in his embrace of crudeness and obscenity, although these accord with the expectations of his contemporary readers. There are moments in Chaucer that might be thought of similarly. Rimbaud also overlaps with trash-punk, especially in moments where he mines and celebrates as poetic the unpoetic qualities of coarseness as well as in the pleasure he takes in presenting himself as an obscene heretic of poetry. But Issa and Catullus worked in traditional forms, and Rimbaud was a lyrical visionary. The overlap here is real, but narrow. Trash-punk is not about the romance of the anti-bourgeois hero, and it is as far from transcendent, private inward dialogue as one could expect to encounter. The historical conditions that would allow this poetry to come into existence wouldn't develop until the beginning of the twentieth century.

The poems associated with trash-punk come out of historical circumstances marked by a predominant and proliferating mass media. This is one of their defining characteristics, and it is the reason why, beyond isolated fragments, examples of this tendency are difficult to find before the turn of the century.

Once culture enters a mass media age, the elements that come together to create trash-punk combine in different ways and in different proportions to produce a poetic chemical reaction. There is an ironic density at work in this, a combination of materials and techniques that, when combined with the catalyst of attitude, allow the elements of a poem to enter into new combinations and produce the trash-punk effect. T. S. Eliot speaks of a related process in *Tradition and the Individual Talent*, one that entails "a more finely perfected medium in which special, or very varied, feelings are at liberty to enter into new combinations. The analogy (is) that of the catalyst."

There is also a question of the editorial threshold that must be crossed in the compiling of this anthology. There is a large field of poetry of the twentieth century that could potentially have been included if the smallest, most granular moments were to be considered—even single lines in otherwise distinct poems. For this reason, I decided on a criterion for inclusion that I call the "51 percent rule." In order to be considered for inclusion, a poem had to reach a threshold of at least 51 percent trash-punk. The ordering of the contributors is chronological by birth date. Because trash-punk passes through many poetry movements over the span of the century, the poems included here don't necessarily represent what the poets are mainly known for.

Trash-punk poems don't behave according to standard literary conceptualizations. There are no masters and imitators here, no programs or dogmatic leaders. It is not a literary movement. It is a wave that passes *through* literary movements, bypassing many common poetic tendencies and transforming others, notably the lapidary tendency—a patrician sense of ornamentation and refinement. The raw poetic ingredients in trash-punk are not rarefied words strung together as expensive jewels connoting high status, but the recombination and transformation of the language that already commonly exists, especially the language of the ordinary, the demotic, and the trashy. It may be that the distinction between jewels and junk becomes beside the point anyway. The corresponding elements of camp—sequins, cheap mascara, and costume jewelry—are junk *and* jewels, rescuing the lapidary from its patrician implications.

In *Notes on "Camp,"* Susan Sontag points out that camp doesn't work simply by inverting judgment of good and bad but by turning its back on the good-bad axis of ordinary aesthetic judgment altogether. To turn one's back on standards of judgment is to broaden the possibility of what can be included in art rather than to create an inverted image of whatever standards of judgment are predominant in any particular era. Trash-punk likewise turns its back on binaries of judgment and seeks out the poetry that can be found in the unique palate of artistic possibilities that results.

Trash-punk poems share a particular kind of pleasure principle with camp sensibility. Overly earnest or sententious work cannot produce this type of pleasure. Sontag points to the viewer's enjoyment of the vulgarity of, for example, a Godzilla movie, where instead of boredom or offense that one might expect from a high-art connoisseur, one finds amusement and delight from the connoisseur of camp. A Japanese monster film like *Rodan* is "touching and quite enjoyable."[1] In this arena of glee, camp and Dada overlap. Kenward Elmslie's poem "Hand" engages in this modality:

> The hand, wizened but sprightly, circled the round toolshed, hunting for Romulus and Remus in what it took to be the total chaos of Outer Space. The dissonance that sounded like time moving backward faster and faster was actually the racket some pals of the Dawn

Brigade (out scrounging for circuits) were making, hurling hard balls of mica at zombies (this is what's so ironic)—victims of amnesia (this is what's so ironic)—but elephant-sized standing in the endless swamp.[2]

Here a swirling mass of wacky psychedelic science-fiction materials mixes freely with zombie movies and lightly dystopian domestic comic-strip sequences.

Russell Atkins's "WEEKEND MURDER" also falls into this category:

> late, suspensed of the hour,
> I seized the beast's buttocks—
> for it's here that sexpants
> spin, convolve, and madden and bedevil!
> and did they scream in fear
> ghastlying the bilged air,
> opprobrious shrilling
> slithering a chair's arms,
> or flustering, thitherd—[3]

Atkins casts these unlikely erotic scenes as a comedic B-movie horror film.

When you watch a Godzilla film, you can be confident that not everyone is going to understand its value, and it is unnecessary to imagine that most people would. In camp sensibility, and to an even greater degree, in trash-punk poems, this confidence is brought a step farther. There is a pleasure taken in the knowledge that other people are *not* likely to enjoy it. This is the pleasure of breaking free of arbitrary social constraints, which is also a punk-rock pleasure. The knowledge that the poetry will cause displeasure in a hidebound reader is part of its value and is an aspect of the delight a responsive reader takes in it. This is a punk-rock attitude that ignores claims of universality. This attitude can be found in the anti-establishment, anti-consumerist, anti-patriarchy part of punk, for instance, in the X-Ray Spex's song "Oh Bondage! Up Yours!"

> Some people think little girls should be seen and not heard
> But I think "oh bondage, up yours!"
> One-two-three-four!
> Bind me, tie me, chain me to the wall
> I wanna be a slave to you all

> Oh bondage, up yours
> Oh bondage, no more
>
> Chain-store chainsmoke, I consume you all
> Chain-gang chainmail, I don't think at all
> Oh bondage, up yours[4]

It also marks a point of intersection with trash sensibility. John Waters points out about his films, "Filth still has a punch to it. The right kind of people understand it and it frightens away the timid." Waters's statement about trash cinema echoes William Blake's aversion to the "tame high finisher of paltry Blots."[5]

One of the things that trash-punk can do that poetry isn't usually supposed to do is deploy an angry affect in a poem. Part of the punk attitude is having the freedom to use anger as an energy. Bruce Andrews's "Eagles Ate My Estrogen" has a John Lydon–like socially charged hostile sneer, using collaged elements featuring abrasively shifting speech registers, insults, exclamations, bodily fluids, and, in general, a plethora of "socially stigmatized" ingredients.[6]

> Yeah man, I'm chick and you're dick
> Darling you're not sperming me on
> Fuck him, fuck them & fuck you
> Take your rubbers around town
> Everything you know is mediocre
> Women do not gain credibility when they get older—therefore, society is fucked
> Mommy, I can't turn off the garbage disposal!
> Big cricket ejaculated under my bed!
> Just because Alan Alda is a feminist doesn't mean he's interesting.
> Every mother's son dips his little weenie into the ink
> Trade your baby for a car[7]

Kathy Acker's "Hello, I'm Erica Jong." uses an angry, corrosive punk sarcasm:

> Hello, I'm Erica Jong. I'm a real novelist. I write books that talk to you about the agony of American life, how we all suffer, the growing pain that more and more of us are going to feel. Life in this country is going to be more horrible, unbearable, making us maniacs cause mania and

death will be the only doors out of prison except for those few rich people and even they are agonized prisoners in their masks, the paths, the ways they have to act to remain who they are. You think booze sex coke rich food etc. are doors out? Temporary oblivion at best. We need total oblivion. What was I saying? Oh, yes, my name is Erica Jong.[8]

The flip side of punk's aggressiveness and abrasiveness is cuteness, a quality found to different degrees in trash-punk poems, often abutting and mixing freely with moments of hostility and irritation. Cuteness is associated with low art—immature or infantile content that would normally be considered too embarrassing to be considered for inclusion in poetry. The punk attitude of not caring what others think about you and doing and including whatever you want in art comes into play here, utilizing not just negative affects but also oddness.

Sianne Ngai classifies cuteness as the aestheticization of powerlessness, pointing out that "a certain kind of avant-garde poetry has helped us better understand the surprising complexity of the cute's overt simplicity, the unsuspected power of its exaggerated powerlessness."[9] If camp is a tender feeling, then there is a related dynamic in cuteness from the tender affection it can incite. Gertrude Stein often uses an odd, cute aesthetic in relation to animals. Adorno points out that animals have a crucial relationship with the role of playfulness in art.

> In its clownishness, art consolingly recollects prehistory in the primordial world of animals. Apes in the zoo together perform what resembles clown routines. The collusion of children with clowns is a collusion with art, which adults drive out of them just as they drive out their collusion with animals. Human beings have not succeeded in so thoroughly repressing their likeness to animals that they are unable in an instant to recapture it and be flooded with joy; the language of little children and animals seems to be the same. In the similarity of clowns to animals, the likeness of humans to apes flashes up; the constellation animal/fool/clown is a fundamental layer of art.[10]

Edith Sitwell, in "Ass-Face," morphs from childlike playfulness to delirious playfulness:

> Ass-Face drank
> The asses' milk of the stars ...
> the milky spirals as they sank
> From heaven's saloons and golden bars,

Made a gown
For Columbine,
Spirting, down
On sands divine
By the asses' hide of the sea
(With each tide braying free).
And the beavers building Babel
Beneath each tree's thin beard,
Said, "Is it Cain and Abel
Fighting again we heard?"
It is Ass-Face, Ass-Face,
Drunk on the milk of the stars,
Who will spoil their houses of white lace—
Expelled from the golden bars![11]

W. B. Yeats, in his *Modern Poetry: A Broadcast*, praises the poem and identifies this mode of Sitwell's as a kind of ludic phantasmagoria where inherited convictions, the presuppositions of thoughts, drop away: "I find her obscure, exasperating, delightful. I think I like her best when she seems a child, terrified and delighted by the story it is inventing.... When you listen to this poem, you should become two people, one a sage who thinks perhaps that Ass-Face is the stupefying frenzy of nature, one a child listening to a poem as irrational as a 'Sing a Song of Sixpence.'"[12]

Stein often engages this sense of childlike play in relation to cuteness and animals.

WHAT DO I SEE?

A very little snail.
A medium sized turkey.
A small band of sheep.
A fair orange tree.
All nice wives are like that.
Listen to them from here.
Oh.
You did not have an answer.
Here.
Yes.[13]

Here the cuteness is delivered with a solid dose of oddness—the punk insistence on representing one's unique weirdness. The syntax also starts to give way in the face of cuteness. Ngai points out that "cuteness does something to everyday communicative speech: weakening or even dissolving syntax and reducing lexicon to onomatopoeia."[14]

The cuteness starts to dissolve the syntax of the poem into something more like a collage or a list. "Cuteness might be described as an aesthetic experience that makes language not just more vulnerable to deformation but also transformation," Ngai says.[15]

Stein will also combine cuteness with maddening repetition:

WHY DO YOU FEEL DIFFERENTLY.

Why do you feel differently about a very little snail and a big one.
Why do you feel differently about a medium sized turkey and a very large one.
Why do you feel differently about a small band of sheep and several sheep that are riding.[16]

The longer this repetition goes on, the more the tone of the poem transforms from the softness of cuteness back into its corresponding punk inverse of agitation and abrasiveness.

The trash-punk dynamic overlaps with punk rock on a broader scale. For the punk-rock listener, the knowledge that their parents will hate it is part of its appeal. What Einstein said about the relativity of time and space, Iggy Pop said about relative judgments of good and bad, remarking, "What sounds to you like a big load of trashy old noise . . . is in fact . . . the brilliant music of a genius, myself." Here Iggy Pop's 1977 insight into the nature of aesthetics enters a stream of thought that includes Aristotle, Hume, and Kant. This is the disharmonious play of imagination and understanding.

The inclusive quality of Sontag's camp sensibility is also important: "What it does is to offer for art (and life) a different—a supplementary—set of standards." Part of the pleasure of trash-punk poetry is the recognition of expanded limits. The "Oh, you can do *that*!" effect. It is the pleasure in the recognition of previously unknown possibilities. This pleasure also implies a speculation about what other possibilities might be right in front of us, unseen.

There is a "badness" necessary to create a camp effect, but it is not just any kind of badness. This badness also has its own signature of ironic density and particular combinations of tone and attitude necessary to achieve activation. There is a good taste of bad taste. There has to be an awareness of the larger binary opposition of good and bad taste to violate rules of taste in the camp sense. When it works, this liberates energy. Camp's staged failure of seriousness opens a path to a particular kind of glee. Trash-punk poetry shares the unpretentiousness and irresponsibly imaginative quality of camp, but for the most part it doesn't use the structure of passionately failed seriousness. Instead, it takes a slightly different path. Rejection of evaluative binaries is not the whole story. One could simply align oneself with the low, the vernacular, and leave it at that, as in a Charles Bukowski poem. But then the binaries would be intact, and the rescue-art part of anti-art wouldn't factor in in the same way. Trash-punk presents a critical edge toward low content as well, partly by applying High Modernist techniques to that content. It mixes things that aren't supposed to be mixed.

The pathos of camp, the friendliness of it, is another strong point of comparison. Sontag points out that camp taste identifies with what it is enjoying: "Camp is a tender feeling."[17] One of her central points is about the process of screening things out, of filtering, and how this can interfere with the process of enjoyment. She's making an argument that it is bad to cheat yourself out of things and that to take an attitude of aligning oneself exclusively with high art is to use a filtering process that is self-defeating, because it involves filtering out different kinds of truths about the human situation. Filtering processes, like opposed binaries of aesthetic judgment, are difficult to get away from, but poetic filtering can be adjusted to use a much wider setting that lets more things through, and binaries can be set aside when the opportunity arises.

If failed seriousness is the central structuring dynamic of camp, then collage is the central structuring dynamic of trash-punk poetry. The materials of Dada were not paint but ripped photographic reproductions, books, newspapers, and stubs—seemingly nonartistic materials that were also the materials being supplied by the mass media. Meant for the garbage can, these materials wound up on the canvas. As mass-media environments became more and more oversaturated with information, collage became a more and more pertinent artistic approach, because the environment itself becomes more collagelike. Collage allows for quick, fluid, dynamic juxtaposition and contrast. This is an approach well suited to a poetry of incongruity, absurdity, and recombination, and it can facilitate, through the ease of reshuffling elements into various new relationships, the destabilization of conventional hierarchies of value. The traditional order of relations between elements is put into a blender with the process of collage, which inherently involves a concatenation of multiple perspectives. Hannah Weiner's book-length poem *Weeks* presents vividly raw juxtapositions of language drawn from TV news transcriptions.

> Police say he's been granted political asylum   For now the radio-active dirt stays where it is   Wild increases will not be permitted The first tall ship arrives in New York for operation op-sail She is wonderful, she is a symbol of freedom   They specialize in hate mongering and hysteria   I'm really impressed with the dedicationof heart teams I felt totally helpless, needy and afraid   6% of psychiatrists admit to having sex with their patients   He owns exotic real estate around the world Bavarian hay is radioactive[18]

In *Weeks*, Weiner transforms the seemingly unpoetic material of TV news language into a densely poetic multiperspective information sculpture.

Collage also creates a field of construction. No matter how destabilizing the particular juxtaposition of elements in a collage are, a parallel coherence and continuity are made manifest in the fact of having reordered these elements into a particular sequence at a particular time and place through the agency of a particular person. One consequence of this is that a poem presenting collaged, contrasting multiple perspectives also becomes a poem with a new perspective comprised of those parts fused into a new compound continuity, a virtual subject position incorporating all of them in some way. Apollinaire's *Monday Rue Christine* is a collage of multiple fragments of conversation overheard on the street made into a text that functions simultaneously as a collection of separate fragments of utterance and as the fusion of separate voices coming together to form a compound, virtual voice. It is a poem of demotic speech edging into the carnivalesque with its comic verbal composition and use of abuse and curses. But it's not simply the demotic or overheard, it's the highly *edited* demotic.

> Three lit gas jets
> The boss has TB

> When you're finished we'll play a game of backgammon
> An orchestra conductor with a sore throat
> When you come to Tunis I'll get you some dope to smoke
>
> That rings a bell
>
> Piles of saucers some flowers a calendar
> Bim bam bim
> Hell I owe 300 francs to my landlady
> I'd rather cut off my dong than pay her[19]

The inclusive quality in camp sensibility is even greater in collage-based art, because collage can potentially include anything. With this theoretically infinite combinatorial potential, the choosing and integrating process involved becomes paramount, and the creative continuum revealed is conducive to a reevaluation of assumptions about the previous relation of the parts. Much of trash-punk poetry exists within this continuum. Collage is a broad process that is common and familiar to everyone because human consciousness itself can be thought of as a kind of collage, with various fragments of information constantly being reshuffled and competing to see what content, what thoughts, come to the surface and in what order. Trash-punk poems do not exist in a remote realm of esoteric literary vanguardism far from everyday experience—they are close to the everyday associative processes of our brains.

If Weiner and Apollinaire present the rawer side of the collage spectrum, then Kenneth Koch presents a more elaborated side, where the writing is paratactic and collaged but also fused into one absurd and hilariously unhinged lyric voice.

> ...O tears
> Of my First Wild Wheel, a laboring thatchery
> Of sea-high, grouped cuffs! navel
> Of the business laboratory, day an orchid's
> Way birth cardinal season-animals
> Went beer fear notification jail-bird machinery
> Of bees like 'gone' whim 'flam' oh inter-'mooped'
> Pathetic lucky badger sea! Meant Wormwood sea

> Of E double interlocutress silk stockings
> Making never seem like yesterday! Oh hop
> How been in the!" "Jane. Hoop moorishness an ridge
> On lilac cubbies." "Orange orange am-I dimple,
> Immersed the whole sea?"[20]

The poems of Clark Coolidge included here create a poetic space of warped comical collage where collisions of excited speech registers fuse into a multi-sided virtual subject.

> the transparent mantids rest on highest knit girders for their nests,
>   tho
> the belted cops have vacated Colorado forever
> Chipmunk Berries kept the "war effort" hung in bulge
>   & fire creeps to cement the mothers flee! (Buy a Kit!)
>   Bee grew a beard! won a prize![21]

This creates a feeling of quirkiness, hilarity, and uncanniness not unlike certain weird, funny moments in David Lynch's *Twin Peaks*. Collage-based poems evoke a feeling of unpredictability, generating microterrains of surprise. This element of collage parallels the surprise built into the structure of humor, the unexpected twist at the end of a joke.

Cult films are often collagelike in their structure, a mélange of outrageous scenes sequenced together in an improbable manner outside the normal spell of reality generated by plausible chronological narrative. Trash cinema steps out of the conventional standards of taste; it also steps outside the spell of reality. In trash, camp sensibility is transmuted into the pathos of travesty. Bad taste is embraced as a source of joy. Something of the ambiguous reception of this unlikely release of repressed energy is captured in a *Detroit Free Press* review of *Pink Flamingos*: "Like a septic tank explosion—it has to be seen to be believed."

Black comedies such as Waters's routinely treat what is normally taken seriously as comedic fodder; this can also be inverted. The Baroness Elsa von Freytag-Loringhoven's "Kindly" is an example of a poem that fits the trash sensibility, a sentimental poem of religious revelation centered on the shifting depiction of the relationship between God and a fart. Following the logic of God as the grand master of creation, it celebrates and traces the radical inclusiveness of this way of thinking to its unlikely yet logical end. The poem appears to be a kind of satire, but there is a genuinely joyous, energized feeling to it, a tone of naïve discovery.

> and God spoke kindly to mine fart
> So kindly spoke He to mine fart
> He said: "Comest from a farting heart!"
> So kindly spoke He to mine fart.
>
> He said:
> "I made—
> The foreparts
> And the hinderparts—
> I made the farts—
> I made the hearts———
> I am the grand master of the arts!"[22]

This is the discovery that God's creative design includes the creation of both farting and screwing, and, beyond that, the fact that God can address a fart in direct, unmediated revelation. It explodes with the joyful comedic effect of an escape from the tyranny of good taste. Satire and irony can imply a superiority to the object being satirized, but this is not the case in "Kindly." It reads as ludicrously and oddly positive. Trash cinema involves a dynamic of making fun of an object that the satirist admires. This creates a leveling effect that parallels the democratic redistribution of related elements in collage. It has a pathos.

Trash aesthetic has its roots in an affection for exploitation films that pointedly avoid displays of redeeming social value as well as in an affection for the performativity of drag aesthetics and what Waters refers to as the white trash culture of Baltimore. As he points out, "I make fun of things I really like. I think that's very important in comedy. Nothing's funny if you make comedy about something you hate. It can be funny for about ten minutes but it doesn't really work unless you love what you're making fun of. I look up to bad taste because it's a freedom I don't have. I do care what people think."[23]

Trash involves both suspended aesthetic judgment and theatrically reversed aesthetic binaries, where different incongruous elements intermingle in a manner that can be appalling as well as affectionate. The elements spill out in unpredictable proportions. Trash involves the successful, contradictory fusion of the charming with the intentionally obnoxious. It fuses charm with what Ngai classifies as "noncathartic," "unprestigious" emotions—hostility grounded in obstructed agency.[24] In this sense trash cinema is also punk-rock cinema. Trash film also strives to entertain audiences by providing a comical shock they haven't experienced before, a process which itself travesties the self-conscious production of novelty common to twentieth-century avant-garde poetry movements.

Trash-punk poetry leads up to the Internet age. It is a wave that passes through a century of poetry movements to reach the present day. The combined elements, sensibilities, and dynamics in play—including suspended or destabilized standards of judgment, collage technique, humor, and parallels to camp, trash, and punk—all lead up to a point where mass media becomes digitized and networked. It leads to Internet-era poetries, such as Flarf, that utilize and reflect the social world of digital mass media. Artistic access to the digital materials of collage and the speed at which those materials can be rearranged has increased exponentially. The common use of the Internet has brought information collage into the realm of everyday life. Eliot, in "Tradition and the Individual Talent," describes how "impressions and experiences combine in peculiar and unexpected ways."[25] In the information age, this process applies not just to the various thoughts, images, and feelings in one poet's mind but also to the simultaneous impressions and experiences of many interconnected minds. Digital networking and computers greatly increase the mobility and the volume of information at the poet's disposal, as well as the exposure to an exploded array of different texts, perspectives, and speech registers from the rarified to the cringeworthy. The Internet has also created a general shift of all cultural access into more collagelike patterns, where access to any part of an artwork or album or movie can easily be fished out of the mass of available material. In the information age, the single stream of consciousness associated with High Modernism becomes multiple streams of consciousness, multiple perspectives colliding and flowing together.

Ron Padgett has spoken about the concept of the "huh?" effect, the intentional elicitation of a feeling of befuddlement from the reader. This playful maneuver engages a pleasure principle, as opposed to an anhedonic alienation effect, to induce a puzzled state of mind. Trash-punk poems are structured so that the receptive reader has to ask questions about them. These poems won't work if the reader approaches them with the intention of being mesmerized by an authoritative master. They make this relationship impossible. This has the effect of altering the imbalance of power between poet and reader, inviting the reader to participate and question even as the poem provides a kind of entertainment. This replaces the model of the writer/reader relation where the reader is positioned to passively admire the poet's display of conquering the medium of language. This also parallels the rebellious democratic three-chord simplicity of punk rock—art that anyone could potentially do.

It's no longer possible to maintain a vision of Modernist poetry as a monolithically difficult and unpleasant vitamin capsule that must be swallowed. Modernist poetry is not just about elevated difficulty and feats of mastery created for a highly trained elect. It can proceed the way punk rock does by radical simplification, such as in the Ramones "I Want to be Sedated":

> Twenty-twenty-twenty four hours to go
> I wanna be sedated
> Nothing to do nowhere to go-o-oh
> I wanna be sedated

Ted Berrigan's minimal, aggressive, one-line poem "Ass-Face" works splendidly in this mode:

> This is the only language you understand, Ass-Face!

This poem reads as language overheard, perhaps on the street—a one-line appropriation that works as a complete poem. It features a minimum of material but a good bit of punk attitude.

Trash-punk can use low or coarsened materials, producing a feeling of provocative, energized rawness. Frank O'Hara points to something similar when he speaks of "life-giving vulgarity." Poetry need not always be treated with great sobriety; it can be vulgar, and it can be absurd. The Residents's general artistic approach of *putting your worst foot forward*, and their alarming absurdist unlikeliness, also overlaps with this, as in "Sinister Exaggerator":

> Your life is leaning downhill, sloping off the outer edge
> Your undetermined oyster beds were found to be a hedge
> You cause the kids of Elmer Fudd to feed the farmer whose
> Cadavers filled with onion rings and feet are filled with glue[26]

So too does the Stein-like maddening repetition combined with inarticulate abjectness pushed to the point of absurdity one finds in Flipper's "Brainwash":

> Um
> Okay, like
> S-see there was this . . .
> And . . . Wh-and then there wa—an—
> Nevermind
> Forget it
> You wouldn't understand anyway[27]

Elsa von Freytag-Loringhoven's "A Dozen Cocktails—Please," with its fast-paced irreverence, could easily read as punk rock lyrics.

> They have dandy celluloid tubes—all sizes—
> Tinted diabolically as a baboon's hind-complexion.
> A man's a—
> Piffle! Will-o'-th'-wisp! What's the dread
> Matter with the up-to-date-American-
> Home-comforts? Bum insufficient for the
> Should-be well groomed upsy!
> That's the leading question.[28]

This poem uses an abrasive, aggressive, unpredictable register, not unlike the song "Forming" by the Germs:

> Over there, the Queen, she says
> Let's stamp them out and dry those tears
> Saturation - we want in taxes
> Flagellation - we've got gashes[29]

Mina Loy's "Songs to Joannes" is an intense, rude, bodily fluid–filled poem that also occupies the punk-lyricism side of the trash-punk spectrum.

> Constellations in an ocean
> Whose rivers run no fresher
> Than a trickle of saliva

    - Pulls a weed white and star-topped
    Among wild oats sewn in mucous-membrane[30]

    The status of the reader's suggestibility is finally thrown into question by the trash-punk aesthetic. This poetry makes it difficult for readers to position themselves as suggestible to poetic mesmerism. It activates or encourages a kind of cognitive flexibility, representing an anti-transcendental tendency. In this sense, it is instructive—by encouraging skepticism toward the social instrumentality of transcendence effects. It acknowledges that thoughts are just temporary mental constructions, discouraging any confusion of words and ideas with reality. It is also satirical on several levels, and because it can include many mixed layers of subjectivity, it can be said to include a kind of lyricism, the lyricism of multiple subjectivities. Trash-punk poems can encompass didactic, satirical, and lyrical modes simultaneously, using a ludic adhesiveness—a sense of play that holds the poem together.

    Poetry takes a position on reality no matter what, even when it does so by inverting values and thereby distancing itself from reality's spell. It can unconsciously and/or consciously object to the conditions of society. But since the conditions of society are also reflected in the systems that produce poems, poetry must also be willing to distance itself from its *own* spell. While bound up in this dialectic, poetry uncovers the poetic values hidden in formerly unpoetic things.

Notes

1. Susan Sontag, *Against Interpretation and Other Essays* (London: Picador, 2001), 285.
2. Kenward Elmslie, *Tropicalism* (Calais, VT: Z Press, 1975), 41.
3. Russell Atkins, *On the Life and Work of an American Master* (Warrensburg, MO: Pleiades Press, 2013), 66.
4. X-Ray Spex, "Oh Bondage! Up Yours!" on *Live at the Roxy Club* (Poly Styrene, 1977).
5. William Blake, *The Complete Poetry and Prose of William Blake* (Norwell, MA: Anchor Press, 1988), 142.
6. Sianne Ngai, *Ugly Feelings* (Cambridge, MA: Harvard University Press, 2007), 349.
7. Bruce Andrews, *EX WHY ZEE* (Bowery, NY: Roof Books, 1995), 31.
8. Kathy Acker, *Essential Acker* (New York: Grove Press, 2002), 148.

9. Sianne Ngai, *Our Aesthetic Categories: Zany, Cute, Interesting* (Cambridge, MA: Harvard University Press, 2015).
10. Theodor W. Adorno, *Aesthetic Theory* (Minneapolis: University of Minnesota Press, 1997).
11. Edith Sitwell, *Collected Poems of Edith Sitwell* (New York: Overlook Press, 2006).
12. W. B. Yeats, *The Collected Works of W. B. Yeats Vol. V: Later Essays* (New York: Scribner, 1994)
13. Gertrude Stein, *A Stein Reader* (Evanston, IL: Northwestern University Press, 1993), 377.
14. Ngai, *Our Aesthetic Categories*.
15. Ngai, *Our Aesthetic Categories*.
16. Stein, *A Stein Reader*.
17. Sontag, *Against Interpretation*, 292.
18. Hannah Weiner, *Weeks* (West Lima, WI: Xexoxial Editions, 2008), 40.
19. Guillaume Apollinaire, *Zone* (New York: NYRB Poets, 2015), 165.
20. Kenneth Koch, *When The Sun Tries To Go On* (Los Angeles: Black Sparrow Press, 1969), 101.
21. Clark Coolidge, *Uncollected and Unpublished Poems* (1962–1968). https://writing.upenn.edu/epc/authors/coolidge/uncoll2.html.
22. Elsa von Freytag-Loringhoven, *Body Sweats: The Uncensored Writings of Elsa von Freytag-Loringhoven* (Cambridge, MA: MIT Press, 2011), 86.
23. John Waters. "Filth 101." YouTube, 2000. https://www.youtube.com/watch?v=qKwVPFMQaHQ.
24. Ngai, *Ugly Feelings*.
25. T. S. Eliot, *Selected Prose of T. S. Eliot* (New York: Ecco, 1975), 37.
26. The Residents, "Sinister Exaggerator," on *Duck Stab EP* (1978).
27. Flipper, "Brainwash," on *Sexbomb Baby* (1981).
28. Freytag-Loringhoven, *Body Sweats*, 48.
29. Germs, "Forming," single (B. Pyn, 1977).
30. Mina Loy, *The Lost Lunar Baedeker* (New York: Farrar, Straus and Giroux, 1997).

Baroness Elsa von Freytag-Loringhoven

Kindly

Inspired by J. J.'s Ulysses

And God spoke kindly to mine heart
So kindly spoke He to mine heart
He said, "Thou art allowed to fart!"
So kindly spoke He to mine heart.

And God spoke kindly to mine fart
So kindly spoke He to mine fart
He said: "Comest from a farting heart!"
So kindly spoke He to mine fart.

He said:
"I made—
The foreparts
And the hinderparts—
I made the farts—
I made the hearts———
I am the grand master of the arts!"

He said:
"Ahee!
I made the oyster shit the pearl—
I made the boy to screw the girl—"
Said He.

A Dozen Cocktails—Please

No spinster—lollypop for me—yes—we have
No bananas—I got lusting palate—I
Always eat them————
They have dandy celluloid tubes—all sizes—
Tinted diabolically as a baboon's hind-complexion.
A man's a—
Piffle! Will-o'-th'-wisp! What's the dread
Matter with the up-to-date-American-
Home-comforts? Bum insufficient for the
Should-be well groomed upsy!
That's the leading question.
There's the vibrator————
Coy flappertoy! I am adult citizen with
Vote—I demand my unstinted share
In roofeden—witchsabbath of our Baby-
Lonian obelisk.
What's radio for—if you please?
"Eve's dart pricks snookums upon
Wirefence."
An apple a day————
It'll come————
Ha! When? I'm no tongueswallowing yogi.
Progress is ravishlng—
It doesn't *me*—
Nudge it—
Kick it—
Prod it—
Push it-—
Broadcast————
That's the lightning idea!
s.o.s. national shortage of——

What ?
How are we going to put it befitting
Lifted upsys?
Psh! Any sissypoet has sufficient freezing
Chemicals in his Freudian icechest to snuff all
Cockiness. We'll hire one.
Hell! Not that! That's the trouble— —
Cock*crow*—silly!
Oh—fine!
They're in France—the air on the line—
The Poles— — — — — —
Have them send waves—like candy—
Valentines— — —
"Say it with— — —
Bolts !
Oh thunder!
Serpentine aircurrents— — —
Hhhhhphssssssss! The very word penetrates!
I feel whoozy!
I like that. I don't hanker after
Billyboys—but I am entitled
To be deeply shocked.
So are we—but you fill the hiatus.
Dear—I ain't queer—I need it straight— —
A dozen cocktails—please— — — —

Subjoyride

READY-TO-WEAR—
AMERICAN SOUL POETRY.
(THE RIGHT KIND)

It's popular—spitting Maillard's
Safety controller handle—
You like it!
They actually kill Paris
Garters dromedary fragrance
Of C. N. in a big Yuban!
Ah—madam—
That is a secret Pep-O-Mint—
Will you try it—
To the last drop?

Tootsie kisses Marchall's
Kippered health affinity
4 out of 5—after 40—many
Before your teeth full-o'
Pep with 10 nuggets products
Lighted Chiclets wheels and
Axels—carrying Royal
Lux Kamel hands off the
Better Bologna's beauty—
Get this straight—Wrigley's
Pinaud's heels for the wise
Nothing so Pepsodent—soothing—
Pussy Willow—kept clean
With Philadelphia Cream
Cheese.
They satisfy the man of
Largest mustard underwear—
No dosing—
Just rub it on.

Weak—rundown man like
The growing miss as well—
Getting on and off unlawful
Will jelly—jam—or Meyer's
Soap noodles
The Rubberset kind abounds—
The exact flavor lasts—
No metal can VapoRub
Oysterettes.

Wenatchee Barbasol peaks
Father John's patent—presentation—
Set—cold—gum's start
And finish.
18 years' electro-pneumatic
Operation Mary Garden cost
The golden key $1,500,000
Smile—see Lee Union—all
It's the grandest thing—
After every meal—no boiling
Required—keeps the
Doctor a day—just Musterole
Dear Mary—the mint with
The hole—oh Lifebouy!
Adheres well—delights
Your taste— continuous
Germicidal action—it
Means a wealth of family
Vicks—
Our men know their
Combatant jobs since 1888
Quicker than Maxwell
Brakes.
You can teach a select
Seal packer parrot—Rinso—
Postum lister World-War
On Saxo Salve— —

Try a venotonic semi-
Soft of a stiff indigestion
Don't scratch!
Original sunshine makes
Tanlac children
Do you know that made
From rich pure shaving
Cream Jim Henry tired
Out?

Famous Fain reduces
Red'lar fellows to the
Toughest Cory Chrome
Pancake apparel—kept
Antiseptic with gold dust
Rapid transit— —
It has raised 3 generations
Of mince-piston-rings-pie.
Wake up your passengers—
Large and small—to ride
On pins— dirty erasers and
Knives
These 3 Graces operate slot
For 5 cents.
Don't envy Aunt Jemima's
Self raising Cracker Jack
Laxative knitted chemise
With the chocolaty
Taste—use Pickles in Pattern
Follow Green Lions.

Gertrude Stein

From *Tender Buttons*

BREAKFAST

A change, a final change includes potatoes. This is no authority for the abuse of cheese. What language can instruct any fellow.

A shining breakfast, a breakfast shining, no dispute, no practice, nothing, nothing at all.

A sudden slice changes the whole plate, it does so suddenly.

An imitation, more imitation, imitation succeed imitations.

Anything that is decent, anything that is present, a calm and a cook and more singularly still a shelter, all these show the need of clamor. What is the custom, the custom is in the centre.

What is a loving tongue and pepper and more fish than there is when tears many tears are necessary. The tongue and the salmon, there is not salmon when brown is a color, there is salmon when there is no meaning to an early morning being pleasanter. There is no salmon, there are no tea-cups, there are the same kind of mushes as are used as stomachers by the eating hopes that makes eggs delicious. Drink is likely to stir a certain respect for an egg cup and more water melon than was ever eaten yesterday. Beer is neglected and cocoanut is famous. Coffee all coffee and a sample of soup all soup these are the choice of a baker. A white cup means a wedding. A wet cup means a vacation. A strong cup means an especial regulation. A single cup means a capital arrangement between the drawer and the place that is open.

Price a price is not in language, it is not in custom, it is not in praise.

A colored loss, why is there no leisure. If the persecution is so outrageous that nothing is solemn is there any occasion for persuasion.

A grey turn to a top and bottom, a silent pocketful of much heating, all the pliable succession of surrendering makes an ingenious joy.

A breeze in a jar and even then silence, a special anticipation in a rack, a gurgle a whole gurgle and more cheese than almost anything, is this an astonishment, does this incline more than the original division between a tray and a talking arrangement and even then a calling into another room gently with some chicken in any way.

A bent way that is a way to declare that the best is all together, a bent way shows no result, it shows a slight restraint, it shows a necessity for retraction.

Suspect a single buttered flower, suspect it certainly, suspect it and then glide, does that not alter a counting.

A hurt mended stick, a hurt mended cup, a hurt mended article of exceptional relaxation and annoyance, a hurt mended, hurt and mended is so necessary that no mistake is intended.

What is more likely than a roast, nothing really and yet it is never disappointed singularly.

A steady cake, any steady cake is perfect and not plain, any steady cake has a mounting reason and more than that it has singular crusts. A season of more is a season that is instead. A season of many is not more a season than most.

Take no remedy lightly, take no urging intently, take no separation leniently, beware of no lake and no larder.

Burden the cracked wet soaking sack heavily, burden it so that it is an institution in fright and in climate and in the best plan that there can be.

An ordinary color, a color is that strange mixture which makes, which does make which does not make a ripe juice, which does not make a mat.

A work which is a winding a real winding of the cloaking of a relaxing rescue. This which is so cool is not dusting, it is not dirtying in smelling, it could use white water, it could use more extraordinarily and in no solitude altogether. This which is so not winsome and not widened and really not so dipped as dainty and really dainty, very dainty, ordinarily, dainty, a dainty, not in that dainty and dainty. If the time is determined, if it is determined and there is reunion there is reunion with that then outline, then there is in that a piercing shutter, all of a piercing shouter, all of a quite weather, all of a withered exterior, all of that in most violent likely.

An excuse is not dreariness, a single plate is not butter, a single weight is not excitement, a solitary crumbling is not only martial.

A mixed protection, very mixed with the same actual intentional unstrangeness and riding, a single action caused necessarily is not more a sign than a minister.

Seat a knife near a cage and very near a decision and more nearly a timely working cat and scissors. Do this temporarily and make no more mistake in standing. Spread it all and arrange the white place, does this show in the house, does it not show in the green that is not necessary for that color, does it not even show in the explanation and singularly not at all stationary.

Idem the Same:
A Valentine to Sherwood Anderson

I knew too that through them I knew too that he was through, I knew too that he threw them. I knew too that they were through, I knew too I knew too, I knew I knew them.

I knew to them.

If they tear a hunter through, if they tear through a hunter, if they tear through a hunt and a hunter, if they tear through different sizes of the six, the different sizes of the six which are these, a woman with a white package under one arm and a black package under the other arm and dressed in brown with a white blouse, the second Saint Joseph the third a hunter in a blue coat and black garters and a plaid cap, a fourth a knife grinder who is full faced and a very little woman with black hair and a yellow hat and an excellently smiling appropriate soldier. All these as you please.

In the meantime examples of the same lily. In this way please have you rung.

WHAT DO I SEE?

> A very little snail.
> A medium sized turkey.
> A small band of sheep.
> A fair orange tree.
> All nice wives are like that.
> Listen to them from here.
> Oh.
> You did not have an answer.
> Here.
> Yes.

A VERY VALENTINE

Very fine is my valentine.
Very fine and very mine.
Very mine is my valentine very mine and very fine.
Very fine is my valentine and mine, very fine very mine and mine is my valentine.

WHY DO YOU FEEL DIFFERENTLY

Why do you feel differently about a very little snail and a big one.
Why do you feel differently about a medium sized turkey and a very large one.
Why do you feel differently about a small band of sheep and several sheep that are riding.
Why do you feel differently about a fair orange tree and one that has blossoms as well.
Oh very well.
All nice wives are like that.

To Be
No Please.
To Be
They can please
Not to be
Do they please.
Not to be
Do they not please
Yes please.
Do they please
No please.
Do they not please
No please.
Do they please.
Please.

If you please.
And if you please.
And if they please
And they please.
To be pleased
Not to be pleased.
Not to be displeased.
To be pleased and to please.

KNEELING

One two three four five six seven eight nine and ten.
The tenth is a little one kneeling and giving away a rooster with this feeling.
I have mentioned one, four five seven eight and nine.
Two is also giving away an animal.
Three is changed as to disposition.
Six is in question if we mean mother and daughter, black and black caught her, and she offers to be three she offers it to me.
That is very right and should come out below and just so.

BUNDLES FOR THEM
A HISTORY OF GIVING BUNDLES

We are able to notice that each one in a way carried a bundle, they were not a trouble to them nor were they all bundles as some of them were chickens some of them pheasants some of them sheep and some of them bundles, they were not a trouble to them and then indeed we learned that it was the principal recreation and they were so arranged that they were not given away, and to-day they were given away.
I will not look at them again.
They will not look for them again.
They have not seen them here again.

They are in there and we hear them again.

In which way are stars brighter than they are. When we have come to this decision. We mention many thousands of buds. And when I close my eyes I see them.

If you hear her snore
It is not before you love her
You love her so that to be her beau is very lovely
She is sweetly there and her curly hair is very lovely
She is sweetly here and I am very near and that is very lovely.
She is my tender sweet and her little feet are stretched out well which is a treat and very lovely
Her little tender nose is between her little eyes which close and are very lovely.
She is very lovely and mine which is very lovely.

ON HER WAY

If you can see why she feel that she kneels if you can see why he knows that he shows what he bestows, if you can see why they share what they share, need we question that there is no doubt that by this time if they had intended to come they would have sent some notice of such intention. She and they and indeed the decision itself is not early dissatisfaction.

IN THIS WAY

Keys please, it is useless to alarm any one it is useless to alarm some one it is useless to be alarming and to get fertility in gardens in salads in heliotrope and in dishes. Dishes and wishes are mentioned and dishes and wishes are not capable of darkness. We like sheep. And so does he.

LET US DESCRIBE

Let us describe how they went. It was a very windy night and the road although in excellent condition and extremely well graded has many turnings and although the curves are not sharp the rise is considerable. It was a very windy night and some of the larger vehicles found it more prudent not to venture. In consequence some of those who had planned to go were unable to do so. Many others did go and there was a sacrifice, of what shall we, a sheep, a hen, a cock, a village, a ruin, and all that and then that having been blessed let us bless it.

Francis Picabia

Chimney Sperm

Translated by Marc Lowenthal

The leg of lamb under the whip of showers in the dung
forgive behind the curtain in a women's convent.
the body of golden symbolic lotions
makes a cross on their buttocks.
Jesus king of astronomy
heart embossed on his chest
like a pawnshop ruby
eating a blood orange.
Priests freaks dessert of lusts
your wealthy clientele slips on human boots.
My penis has the shape of my heart
on the pillows.
Fondling what a sickness
but you'll come back soon, won't you?
A naked man is never poor
especially if he has politely lost sleep.
You have to jump up my darling and rape your son
onanism is a theory of gestures
that shrivels up the skinflute.
Joan of Arc ink bottle.
I want to tease you reader
not too much.
I've never seen women under a bed
able to raise their legs between their breasts.
I beg of you leave me
I want to make you fold your loins lady readers

terrible teases
I'm going to whip your senses.
I blow under the blankets
I smother the pussy enveloping my hand
I don't really know why these scenes resemble rags.
I kiss your mouth while vomiting.
Death must be an exquisite thing.
I am long.

1st P.S.

The humidity of night lights
rubs out the super-royal writing paper.
A chalice dressed in red has no air.
A fat brunette at the medical school
takes an albino's dick
very bored with this dickhead
she goes back to examining the street.

2nd P.S.

Let's be ridiculous pushed from high up
close to studious candles.
No photographic courage
our hair shall turn white from well-mannered tortures
I love hazelnuts.

3rd P.S.

Bismuth of organs the horoscope of conquests
settled onto a person's dress
pampas bronchitis talking to itself—
It's Tristan Tzara "the fabric clerk"
of Romanian nationality, who found the word DADA.

Pablo Picasso, Juan Gris, your cubist colleagues claim that you took everything from them: that's indeed the impression they give me!
FRANCIS PICABIA THE FUNNY GUY

Apollinaire

Monday rue Christine

Translated by Ron Padgett

The concierge's mother and the concierge will let anything go by
If you're a man you'll go with me tonight
All we'd need is one guy to hold the main door
While the other one goes up

Three lit gas jets
The boss has TB
When you're finished we'll play a game of backgammon
An orchestra conductor with a sore throat
When you come to Tunis I'll get you some dope to smoke

That rings a bell

Piles of saucers some flowers a calendar
Bim bam bim
Hell I owe 300 francs to my landlady
I'd rather cut off my dong than pay her

I leave at 8:27 p.m.
Six mirrors look back and forth at themselves endlessly
I think it's going to get even more confused
Dear Sir
You're a joke
That lady holds more food than a garbage can
Louise forgot her fur
Well I don't even have a fur and I'm not cold

The Dane smokes his cigarette over a timetable
The black cat crosses the bar
Those crêpes were marvelous
The faucet is running
Dress black like her fingernails
It's completely impossible
Here you are sir
The malachite ring
The floor is strewn with sawdust
So it's true
The red-headed waitress ran away with a bookseller

A newspaperman I know only very slightly

Listen Jacques I have something very serious to say to you

Passengers and cargo

He says to me Sir would you care to see what I can do in
    the way of etchings and paintings
I have only one small maid

After lunch Café du Luxembourg

Once there he introduces me to this big fat fellow
Who says
Listen, it's charming
In Smyrna in Naples in Tunis
But where in the name of God is that
The last time I was in China
Eight or nine years ago
Honor often depends on what time of day it is
The royal flush

Mina Loy

from Songs to Joannes

1

    Spawn   of   Fantasies
    Silting the appraisable
    Pig Cupid   his rosy snout
    Rooting erotic garbage
    "Once upon a time"
    Pulls a weed   white and star-topped
    Among wild oats   sewn in mucous-membrane

    I would   an   eye in a bengal light
    Eternity in a sky-rocket
    Constellations in an ocean
    Whose rivers run no fresher
    Than a trickle of saliva

    These   are suspect places

    I must live in my lantern
    Trimming subliminal flicker
    Virginal   to the bellows
    Of Experience
               Coloured   glass

Crab-Angel

1

An atomic sprite
perched on a polished
    monster-stallion
reigns over Ringling's   revolving
trinity of circus attractions

Something the contour
of a captured crab
waving its useless pearly claws

From a squat body
pigmy arms
and bowlegs
with their baroque calves
curve in a bi-circular attitude
to a ballerina's ecstasy

An effigy of Christmas Eves
smile-cast among chrysanthemum curls
it seems a sugar angel—
while from a rose-flecked ruff of gauze
its manly legs
stamp on the vast rump of the horse

An iridescent speck
dripped from a rainbow
onto an ebony cloud

Crab-Angel   I christen you
miniken of masquerade sex

Helen of Lilliput?
Hercules in a powder puff?

2. *(Song)*

"Had you been born
in regions of the Unicorn
To balance on his ivory horn
perhaps"
"Per Bacco! 'Tis an idiot dwarf
hooked to a wire to make him jump"

Automaton bareback rider
the circus-master
jerks
your invisible pendulence
from an overhead pulley
to your illusory
leaps in up-a-loft

signs
the horse
racing the orchestra
in rushing show
throw
his whimsy wire-hung dominator

to dart
through circus skies of arc-lit dust
Crab-Angel   like a swimming star

clutching the tail end of the Chimera

An aerial acrobat
floats on the coiling lightning
of the whirligig

lifts
to the elated symmetry of Flight

A startled rose
whirls in the chaos of the hoofs

The jeering jangling
jazz
crashes to silence

The dwarf
subsides like an ironic sigh
to the soft earth
and ploughs
his bowlegged way
laboriously   towards the exit
waving a yellow farewell with his perruque

William Carlos Williams

The Hermaphroditic Telephones

Warm rains
wash away winter's
hermaphroditic telephones

whose demonic bells
piercing the torpid
ground

have filled with circular
purple and green
and blue anemones

the radiant nothing
of crystalline
spring.

Breakfast

Twenty sparrows
on

a scattered
turd:

Share and share
alike.

Hey Red!

There are men and
plenty of them
whose heads resemble
nothing so much as
the head of a dick—
color and form—
America is full
of them, a kind of
brains I suppose
at that . Thick .

Edith Sitwell

Ass-Face

Ass-Face drank
The asses' milk of the stars...
the milky spirals as they sank
From heaven's saloons and golden bars,
Made a gown
For Columbine,
Spirting, down
On sands divine
By the asses' hide of the sea
(With each tide braying free).
And the beavers building Babel
Beneath each tree's thin beard,
Said, "Is it Cain and Abel
Fighting again we heard?"
It is Ass-Face, Ass-Face,
Drunk on the milk of the stars,
Who will spoil their houses of white lace—
Expelled from the golden bars!

Richard Huelsenbeck

End of the World

Translated by Ralph Manheim

This is what things have come to in this world
The cows sit on the telegraph poles and play chess
The cockatoo under the skirts of the Spanish dancer
Sings as sadly as a headquaters bugler and the cannon lament all day
That is the lavender landscape Herr Mayer was talking about
when he lost his eye
Only the fire department can drive the nightmare from the drawing-
room but all the hoses are broken
Ah yes Sonya they all take the celluloid doll for a changeling
and shout: God save the king
The whole Monist Club is gathered on the steamship Meyerbeer
But only the pilot has any conception of high C
I pull the anatomical atlas out of my toe
a serious study begins
Have you seen the fish that have been standing in front of the
opera in cutaways
for the last two days and nights . . . ?
Ah ah ye great devils—ah ah ye keepers of bees and commandments
With a bow wow wow with a boe woe woe who today does not know
what our Father Homer wrote
I hold peace and war in my toga but I'll take a cherry flip
Today nobody knows whether he was tomorrow
They beat time with a coffin lid
If only somebody had the nerve to rip the tail feathers
out of the trolley car it's a great age
The professors of zoology gather in the meadows

With the palms of their hands they turn back the rainbows
the great magician sets the tomatoes on his forehead
Again thou hauntest castle and grounds
The roebuck whistles the stallion bounds
(And this is how the world is this is all that's ahead of us)

Abraham Lincoln Gillespie

A Poem From Puzlit

sardonically towers

ghoubrel

i shing my ostracization

come back!

come back, I implore you

no—stay away

here

i am ecstaticly.

Tristan Tzara

from Dada Manifestos

Translated by Ralph Manheim

VIII

To make a Dadaist poem
Take a newspaper.
Take a pair of scissors.
Choose an article as long as you are planning to make your poem.
Cut out the article.
Then cut out each of the words that make up this article and put them in a bag.
Shake it gently.
Then take out the scraps one after the other in the order in which they left the bag.
Copy conscientiously.
The poem will be like you.
And here you are a writer, infinitely original and endowed with a sensibility that is charming though beyond the understanding of the vulgar.

Example:
when the dogs cross the air in a diamond like the ideas and the appendix of the meninges shows the hour of awakening program (the title is my own) price they are yesterday agreeing afterwards paintings / appreciate the dream epoch of the eyes / pompously than recite the gospel mode darkens / group the apotheosis imagine he said fatality power of colors / cut arches flabbergasted the reality a magic spell / spectator all to efforts from the it is no longer 10 to 12 /

during digression volt right diminishes pressure / render of madmen topsy-turvy flesh on a monstrous crushing scene / celebrate but their 160 adepts in not to the put in my mother-of-pearl / sumptuous of land bananas upheld illumine / joy ask reunited almost / of has the one so much that the invoked visions / of the sing this one laughs / destiny situation disappears describes this one 25 dances salvation / dissimulated the whole of it is not was / magnificent the ascent to the gang better light of which sumptuousness scene me music-hall / reappears following instant shakes to live / business that there is not loaned / manner words come these people

Metal Coughdrops

Translated by Jerome Rothenberg

her bare feet tell the neurasthenic: fake moustaches on that ostrich made in u.s.a
the cold bird tells the monocle: mouth got no lips I'll kill myself
but the cubist tells the cubist: i have invented the chief-of-scratch &
    I am his boss
the boss tells the boss: boss

Bern Porter

"What's filling lake Michigan faster than waste? Algae."

What's filling lake Michigan faster than waste? Algae.

Was there life before life? Quite probably.

What's the recipe for tea some Ecuadorian Indians use? Brew d-tetrahydroharmine with harmaline and harmine.

How many languages does man speak? About 2,800.

What does it mean when an American wine is labeled Burgundy? Only that it is red.

Where can you get eleven inches of rain in one storm? Arizona.

> What do lightning water, Ethiopian supermarkets, microspheres, Mineral King Valley, twisters, Moslem housewives, firefly trees, Tis Abbai Falls, pond ice, aborigine cookouts, prehistoric sculpture, Indian immolations, pipefish, and mammalian retinas look like? How does a wolf look when he's bored? A polar bear when he's taking a cat nap? A dolphin when he giggles?

Sun Ra

Nuclear War

Nuclear War (yeaaah). Nuclear War (yeaaah)
They're talking about (yeaaah) nuclear war (yeaaah) (x2)

It's a motherfucker, don't you know?
They're talking about nuclear war (yeaaah)
They're talking about (yeaaah) nuclear war (yeaaah)
It's a motherfucker, don't you know?
If they push that button, your ass has got to go (x3)

They're talking about (yeaaah) nuclear war (yeaaah)
They're talking about (yeaaah) nuclear war (yeaaah)
If they push that button your ass has got to go.
They'll blast you so high in the sky
Gonna blast you so high in the sky
You'll kiss your ass goodbye
You'll kiss your ass goodbye
You'll kiss your ass goodbye goodbye

If they push that button. (If they push that button)
You can kiss your ass goodbye goodbye (You can kiss your ass goodbye
    goodbye)

If they push that button (If they push that button)
If they push that button (If they push that button)
If they push that button (If they push that button)
If they push that button (If they push that button)
You can kiss your ass (You can kiss your ass) goodbye goodbye

They're TALKing about (They're TALKing about)
NUCLEAR war (NUCLEAR war)
RadiAtion (RadiAtion). MUtation (MUtation).
RadiAtion (RadiAtion). MUtation (MUtation).
Fire. (Fiiiire). Fire. (Fiiiire).
Hydrogen bombs (Hydrogen bomb). Atomic bombs (Atomic bombs)
Kiss your ass (Kiss your ass) goodbye (goodbye)

If they push that button. (If they push that button)
IT'S A MOTHERFUCKER. (IT'S A MOTHERFUCKER)
DON'T YOU KNOW? (DON'T YOU KNOW?)x2

If they push that button. (If they push that button)
Your ass has got to go. (Your ass has got to go)

IT'S A MOTHERFUCKER. (IT'S A MOTHERFUCKER)
DON'T YOU KNOW? (DON'T YOU KNOW?) (x2)

IF THEY PUSH THAT BUTTON (IF THEY PUSH THAT BUTTON)
YOUR ASS HAS GOT TO GO (YOUR ASS HAS GOT TO GO)

WHAT YOU GONNA DO? (WHAT YOU GONNA DO?)
WITHOUT YOUR ASS? (WITHOUT YOUR ASS?)
WHAT YOU GONNA DO? (WHAT YOU GONNA DO?)
WITHOUT YOUR ASS? (WITHOUT YOUR ASS?)

If they push that button.
MuTAtion (MuTAtion). RadiAtion(RadiAtion)
MuTAtion (MuTAtion). RadiAtion(RadiAtion)
If they push that button.

Fire (Fire). Meltiiiiing (Meltiiiiing). Peoooooople (Peoooooople).
Buiiiiiildings (Buiiiiiildings,), Burnt graaaaass (Burnt graaaaass)

If they push that button (If they push that button)
It's gonna blast you so high. (It's gonna blast you so high).
Up in the sky (Up in the sky).
If they push that button
Kiss your ass goodbye.

Jackson Mac Low

Asymmetry 372

THE INDICATOR HERE!!
                                  ELECTRICAL IMPULSES!

HERE!!
      ELECTRICAL IMPULSES!
                              REMAIN HERE
      ELECTRICAL IMPULSES!

ELECTRICAL IMPULSES!
                              LINGERED THERE TWO MONTHES!

Asymmetry 497

whirr?
   Ames!

     Agamogenesis—
        offering?
           Tuam(- - - - - - - - -
- - - - -)otu Archipelago!
      DON RICKLES:
       Suspense accoun(- - - - - - - -
- - - - -)t Caen,
    Luxenbourg Palace!

   Them,
     right triangle,
   ideogram . . .
        corrosive (- - - - - - - - - - - -
- - - - -)*sublimate:*
     pebble leather:
         thio(- - - - - - - - - - -
- - - - -)antimonious acid.
       TACK?

2nd Light Poem: For Diane Wakoski—10 June 1962

I.

Old light & owl-light
may be opal light
in the small
orifice
where old light
& the will-o'-the-wisp
make no announcement of waning
light

but with direct directions
& the winking light of the will-o'-the-wisp's accoutrements
& lilac light
a delightful phenomenon
a delightful phenomenon of lucence & lucidity needing no
    announcement
even of lilac light
my present activities may be seen in the old light of my accoutrements
as a project in owl-light

II.

A bulky, space-suited figure
from the whole cloth of my present activities
with a taste for mythology in opal light
& such a manner

in the old light from some being outside

as if this being's old light cd have brought such a manner
to a bulky, space-suited figure

from the whole world of my present activities
at this time
when my grief gives owl-light
only
not an opal light
& not a very old light

neither
old light nor owl-light
makes it have such a manner about it
tho opal light & old light & marsh light & moonlight
& that of the whole world
to which the light of meteors is marsh light
all light it
no it's
an emerald light
in the light from the eyes that are making it whole from the whole
    cloth
with no announcement this time.

III.

What is extra light?
A delightful phenomenon.
A delightful phenomenon having no announcement?
No more than the emerald light has.
Is that the will-o'-the-wisp?
No, it's the waning light of my grief.
Is it a winking light?
No more than it is the will-o'-the-wisp.
Is it old light?
The oldest in the whole world.
Why do you speak in such a manner?
I suppose, because of the owl-light.
Is it a kind of opal light?
No, I said it was old light.

Is it a cold light?
More like a chemical light with the usual accoutrements.
Like the carmine light produced by my present activities?
More of a cold light than that.
Like what might fall on a bulky, space-suited figure?
Well, it's neither red light nor reflected light.
Are you making this up out of the whole cloth?
No, I'm trying to give you direct directions.
For avoiding a bulky, space-suited figure?
No, for getting light from a rhodochrosite.

Note: A rhodochrosite is a vitreous rose-red or variously colored gem-stone having a hardness of 4.5 & a density of 3.8 & consisting of manganous carbonate ($MnCO^3$) crystallized in the rhombohedral system.

IV.

This time I'm going to talk about red light.
First of all, it's not very much like emerald light.
Nevertheless, there's still some of it in Pittsburgh.
It adds to the light from eyes an extra light.
This is also true of emerald light.
But red light better suits those with a taste for mythology.
As reflected light it is often paler than the light from a rhodochrosite.
Such a red light might fall on a bulky, space-suited figure.
In just such a manner might this being be illuminated during a time gambol.

40TH DANCE—GIVING FALSELY—22 March 1964

Many begin by getting insects.

Then many make thunder though taking pigs somewhere,
& many give a simple form to a bridge
while coming against something or fearing things.

A little later, after making glass boil
& having political material get in,
many, while being in flight,
name things.

Then many have or seem to have serious holes,
& many question many;
many make payments to many,
& many seem to put exampies up.

Finally many quietly chalk a strange tall bottle.

A Lack of Balance But Not Fatal

A motion guided a lotion
in hiding from a tint
reckless from nowhere enforcement.

A label persisted. The past tense
implies it took place. The redness
in which the the implies there was some other
did not persist. He was not waiting long.

The sentence is not always a line
but the stanza is a paragraph.

The whiteness was not enforced.
it was not the other but another
circumstance brought in the waterfall
while a breath waited without being clear
or even happier. A seal was lost without it.

There was a typical edge. The paper tilted
or even curved. A rattle smoothed its way.
Where the predominance stopped was anyone's guess
but the parrot fought for it with forbearance
and a waiting cart was leashed to a trial
though a lie would have done as well
or even better when a moderate sleeve was cast.

No claim was made. A tired park gained.
A lack twisted the bread. Heads foamed.
Nowhere was little enough for the asking.
The task he cleared from the temperature
was outside the extended account. Each the
points to an absence. One or more hiding.

He asked where the inches were. The could have gone.

Intentions are mixed without quotations.
The song was snug. Ambiguity does not
hang in the air. The space between graphemes
is neither colorless nor tasteless. A stream
runs rapidly in no more history. The sweep
of a line. Kindness is not mistaken
for tinder and the lid is resting but shortness
guarantees no sentence authenticity.

Where the schoolyard was evident a closed
flutter shoed a notion without resistant
fences or a paradox without feathers.
Swiftness outlasts the pencil. A cormorant
rose against a born backdrop. Letters inch.
An iconoclast was hesitant. a fire lit.
In the tank a fire lozenge disengages. Swarms
roared. A special particle felt its form.
Lagging features left oak divination without
a tone or a creased sentinel. Leavings swept.

Toward evening the watchful clock was situated.
No diver called for ether. Lynxes thrived.
Hit by something a silence willed. Streets
were not concerned. A past participle's
sometimes mistaken for a past. An orange
roster was on everybody's mind though clues
could be found. When the ink is incomplete
every table rests on its opposite. A closed
restraint impinged. Furniture rested. Several
pinks in a fist. A clearly charismatic
hideout was read. Neatness wavered. The flag
was wet without exertion or favor. That judge postponed.

Snowfall abused ermines. A folding chair.
Close to the bank a trap was silted though the finder
relaxed without particulars or the least inclination.
Whoever loosened the torrent concluded the tryst.
Finally is the way to find the place. Earshot
is likely. Tones harvest commonplace weather.
The pastness of the past was included in a doctrine
or stakes were wrought. Or sought. Find divers.
Fists rested on the divined peculiarity. Artemis hushed.

Twigs were not grapes. He grasped the tale ring.
Smoothing the horses the clutter died. Finches
sowed roses on the mustered aggregate. Loaves flew.
A mentality ran farther and its crests simmered.
Closeted without bargains the lean rump beheld
no future. A certain flight beckoned. The wonder.
Closed classrooms risk warmth though causation
matters less. Never ink a connection when a plea
is off. Softer dollars were a range without flutters
though a concessive subordinator turns a sentence
into a scene. Dreams were not what he wanted.

16 Jan 1982 New York City

Taylor Mead

From *On Amphetamine and in Europe*

I was married in a
Grecian cathedral to
Prince Peter Ilyitch Groinovosky
attended by 12 hand jobs
and a best man
who put on the ring
and my nipples lactated
and the bands played
the Band-aid waltz
and we rode through
Athens lactating and
waving to the fairy queen
mother who waved back
and shed tears which were
put on with a phony
sponge but the peasants
believed them and we
had 12 years of peace
except for an earthquake.
Now we are entering
middle-age and I would
like a divorce

Can you arrange it

Dea
th

"Why sure."

My space program
is your space because
we all have to go to
the moon sometime
during the day.

*

I dig over-exposures

*

I have been over-exposed
all my life

*

rabbits are eating my underwear

Kenneth Koch

Everyone Is Endymion

1

For the two night of my tea nights
Rattrap shop
Hee, he: mouse, supper, and testament,
Column, laying abstractions,
Lemons, pyramid, algebra, and lids
A metropolitan oafness of labor
Fast adhering to light's zone
Asks you to be within socks on
By Rhone-light, a sea of custom
Landslides, fit and pains
Vastly: land, chiffon peanuts,
Nails, pirate, illness, pier-red parks.
She says, "You got me this way sobbing,
Yet all my finds have friends.
At least you can poach me."
Of constancy her landslide by hats.
Such ones met out with hearts
In my love's town, a kangaroo, an ostrich.

2

The blue beer of disunion
United their leading parts
In sanity, and "I" screamed,
"The housekeeper is wet paints
In cure
Crew," when death-adventurer came,
With bears, Afton, burning parts.

O sables, bedroom
Necklaces, and pinch, safe,
Lorry, billboard, asp, and faculty
Limpets, grass, laymen with coffee:
"Didn't we act stupid without our chairs
In the fashion, this afternoon,
Beneath the tree-bellows of everyone?"

Gypsy Yo-yo

There are ban-dares of "lame" low
Beside "tree" entrance. Hint. Barricades
He ogle. Are the bleeding lifesavers?
Rent hippopotamus! Ave.
Talked savage. In
Says on emp. out
Care, as! bed; free auto tires
Coat, on'd am, O box "e'en" blouse.

No Job at Sarah Lawrence

O woebegone snowflakes, a million cold tablets, alas! merry hat,
    merry commonplace, take place Nan marriage is show business
Parade grounds O peace, winter carriage ocean phenomena eagle
    rain
Banister. Shy people! Europe dent flake easily Montanas
Sherry. Leaf, O loom! seldom
Beside the Greekish wood
A normless kind sweeping dintless carriage
"Moften" would appear. She peaks
Grapes, lines! Man
Toppled, de oh ho yo ho, canary C-foot forests, at now
Oh, harbour; extra lines
Ring at tea foot and certain cows, Oh the bottom
Of a series! how green, camphor, foot ball, Elmer, sing, elbow, sand
    runners, Mediterranean
Armament of tea!

Long long ago, amid the coastlines' breastline magic
Slantline briefcase's
Sweetheart coop llama and sphinx production
O pagans! hear,
Whore, naturalism, simplicity, seduction, amphitheatre,

January, milkmen, hopelessness, and, stare!
Try idea, it is modern, cigars! If blankets
Mutter in cargo, defrayed chests'
Anagram, O coconuts, jujube, and lingo!

Lady, my jungle.
How fond you are of illness,
Elevation, comedy crash beep hooray
Call "ness," life. Sacrilege
Is gnome silver umpire tam, sin,
Sweet to you! Baden
Baden! Lily petals.

We.
Backed through Tulsa, wintry, China's, freshman
Whose queer remark on everything we noticed
Was "Comedy eagle January meditation forehead."
Weird freshman come true delightful rosy night
Sand jumping Samothrace. O peculiar! language,
Scat, rhumba, trireme, manx, silverware, hoop forget! Bogs
Ladylike as the "perfeeect" hornet! Carpet repairs! Oh!
Save me! logs, "hay-pron," forehead, -sail, oh, of slim

Calcium!

from When The Sun Tries To Go On

Bandana of cavey sea-tins! pyjamas! ladder on
"Eek's" bugle call of shallow GLUE, PIER, SOLDIER, and
SPILLWORT dirtiest case of the marshmallow
Sin language, merchantmarine of chows! Back, lurid
Leaf of the Chair FINANCE! O
Santa Claus can heaps behoove love cemetery
Gypsy. Market of playing Beans' Research, Baa
Lethal tagsheep. Erp. "Kill my shabby
Dog with careless BEANS. Or jellybeans
Will complicate four research-
Pilgrims in, lazier than the, GREEN
Rebus of opium. Oh, daze!" Why shirts came RED
As youth ex-Canadas, shallow doggest dream
Lamp, "Sunday I boxed a COLITIS pinprick,
Shore!" Ugh-row of the lazy-towels-when,
GERMANY and CALIFORNIA again! The RIGHT
Beans hill know a banjo toga-conference
Disinterest. Sherman for president! Surface
Chow, O Green! air, go away. BATTERS
Up! "She decides to become the climate
Of ARABIA, she bannisters two CALIFORNIA and
Diamonds. Sense-tea-wear bay dun off oof focus
And becomes WELL-BEING, the turtle
Of grace, knickers, and cactus. SHE has no colitis!"

No wonder! parachuting germ hay-mow squad and king
Every ant is king! minnesingers in gown-
Boxes, ladies, money: WE
Childhood sew. weak ladder peppermint Balkans
Every mind is king! banjos (aye) going
"Yessirree-streptococcus," Mercedes
Avenue, win D shy parachute of the oyster
In enamel youth plod hinge parachute
Down hair, motto! Boled parrallelo-
Grams, weaver is not king! Jaded, though
Mild ands ant, blotter, yoyo ships sate Jericho believers
Angevine "Sewn in his car,
Loosely, amid the raspberries,"—hokku! revolver!
"Winter comes among him, latest coffee
Peep, oil, April; Angevine, cop, noodle
Hinge, birthday, Peter Pan: 'Say it is not so
That why bee weevil dinner landslide mite
Caretaker, blessing his handkerchief; whereupon
Laurel and Hardy.' " Certainly tomorrow is weapon
Pleonasm. Dancing, like kosher icewater
Lays. Rob the conceited strawberry, engine
Count on the deceitful oyster. Imagine the
Sea, that knights! Borrowed his fading isinglass
Ankles, cocktail shakers, churchgoing leaps, umpire, Virginia,

Romance! under fields! one sorghum powder keg
Of chafey golflinks marry to barracuda
Leftwing childhood Santa Claus pyramid lilac
Birthplace changing Eskimo! Snuffing those pears
"Lately I advanced hats eskimo. O tears
Of my First Wild Wheel, a laboring thatchery
Of sea-high, grouped cuffs! navel
Of the business laboratory, day an orchid's
Way birth cardinal season-animals
Went beer fear notification jail-bird machinery
Of bees like 'gone' whim 'flam' oh inter-'mooped'
Pathetic lucky badger sea! Meant Wormwood sea
Of E double interlocutress' silk stockings
Making never seem like yesterday! Oh hop
How been in the!" "Jane. Hoop moorishness an ridge
On lilac cubbies." "Orange Orange am-I dimple,
Immersed the whole sea?" Joke! Wish! Paintbrushes, toe,
Alabaster! "Onto which grotto and a sea-brush lemons
Chair-face gin-ear-all's matting time and Inca of
Careful soda shutting chair-faces oyster shooting
Dane-way of mirrors loons ant, 'arf-woof'
Of British gleeb, the 'nembus' of 'son-away'
Curfews' and naily kerchiefs of demon curlews'
Map-opping 'para-kiffs' grandmother. Is hen"

Frank O'Hara

Fantasy

>   Dedicated to the health of Allen Ginsberg
>   1964

How do you like the music of Adolph
                              Deutsch? I like
it, I like it better than Max Steiner's. Take his
score for *Northern Pursuit*, the Helmut Dantyne theme
was...
            and then the window fell on my hand. Errol
Flynn was skiing by. Down
                          down down went the grim
grey submarine under the "cold" ice.
                                     Helmut was
safely ashore, on the ice.
                          What dreams, what incredible
fantasies of snow farts will this all lead to?
                                               I
don't know, I have stopped thinking like a sled dog.

The main thing is to tell a story.
                                   It is almost
very important. Imagine
                        throwing away the avalanche
so early in the movie. I am the only spy left
in Canada,
           but just because I'm alone in the snow
doesn't necessarily mean I'm a Nazi.
                                     Let's see,
two aspirins a vitamin C tablet and some baking soda

should do the trick, that's practically an
                              Alka
Seltzer. Allen come out of the bathroom
                                   and take it.
I think someone put butter on my skis instead
of wax.
           Ouch. The leanto is falling over in the
firs, and there is another fatter spy here. They
didn't tell me they sent
                         him. Well, that takes care
of him, boy were those huskies hungry.
                                       Allen,
are you feeling any better? Yes, I'm crazy about
Helmut Dantyne
                   but I'm glad that Canada will remain
free. Just free, that's all, never argue with the movies.

Russell Atkins

WEEKEND MURDER

sex pants are what she wears:
each night she tightens them on,
leaves with a flaunt   sexpants
have to be taken by surprise,
they are so uncannily aware

when she's asleep, they're up
convulsing with energy   I've
stealth'd but to behold them
out at night when closets
have long hushed to shut
—despicable twists
lewd'd across hangers

wasn't long, and I had them,
these sexpants, under a shower
           for wet sexpants
are powerless
               sun up'd
she asked, "Where are my pants?
Yes, the blue ones?"

       (had they but drowned!
not on your life!) and she,
she dried them to a starch,
tightened them on and forth'd
left with a flaunt (sex pants
not only have to be surprised,
they must be slain)

late, suspensed of the hour,
I seized the beast's buttocks—
for it's here that sex pants
spin, convolve, and madden and bedevil!
and did they scream in fear
ghastlying the bilged air,
opprobrious shrilling
slithering a chair's arms,
or flustering, thitherd—

I compelled them down
and with a blunt oblong
bashed   I bashed them
      to a squish!

John Ashbery

Leaving the Atocha Station

The arctic honey blabbed over the report causing darkness
And pulling us out of there experiencing it
he meanwhile... And the fried bats they sell there
dropping from sticks, so that the menace of your prayer folds...
Other people...   flash
the garden are you boning
and defunct covering... Blind dog expressed royalties...
comfort of your perfect tar grams nuclear world bank tulip
Favorable to   near the night pin
loading formaldehyde. the table torn from you
Suddenly   and we are close
Mouthing the root   when you think
generator   homes enjoy leered

The worn stool blazing   pigeons from the roof
           driving tractor to squash
Leaving the Atocha Station   steel
infected bumps the screws
    everywhere   wells
abolished top ill-lit
scarecrow falls   Time, progress and good sense
strike of shopkeepers dark blood
no forest you can name drunk scrolls
the completely new Italian hair...
Baby... ice falling off the port
The centennial   Before we can

                    old   eat
members with their chins
              so high up   rats
        relaxing the cruel discussion
    suds   the painted corners
white   most aerial
        garment crow
                    and when the region took us back
the person left us like birds
    it was fuzz on the passing light
over disgusted heads, far into amnesiac
permanent house depot   amounts he can
        decrepit mayor ...   exalting flea
for that we turn around
experiencing it is not to go into
the epileptic prank forcing bar
to borrow out onto tide-exposed fells
over her morsel, she chasing you
and the revenge he'd get
establishing the vultural over
rural area cough protection
murdering quintet. Air pollution terminal
the clear fart genital enthusiastic toe prick album serious evening flames
the lake over your hold   personality
            lightened ...   roar
You are freed
            including barrels
head of the swan   forestry
the night and stars fork
That is, he said
    and rushing under the hoops of
equations probable

        absolute mush   the right
entity   chain store   sewer opened their books
        The flood dragged you
        I coughed to the window
last month: juice, earlier
like the slacks   to be declining
    the peaches   more
  fist
sprung expecting the cattle
false loam   imports
        next time around

Hannah Weiner

from **Weeks**

18

This is invisible stuff up there   Folks were just lying around on the grass   This year we have carefully added new titles not previously available to a national audience as well as selecting titles from last year's list of publishers   Does a healthy body mean a healthy mind   The Soviets have vastly understated their losses   We've got nuclear trucking going through our city Ham radio is always used in the initial stages of a disaster There is fear of loss of face and world opinion and the space program will go on   We're here on 67th St and Lexington Ave. That international aid be allowed into the Ukraine   An expert on bone marrow transplant   Perhaps he will offer them access to the American list   The documents were found in the national archive in Washington   A resistance to the hiring of gays on the part of the membership   How do we know some of those haven't infiltrated the police dept.   They're disgracing the job   The crunch comes when the issue goes public U. S. oil companies or their subsidiaries still pump most of Libya's oil Radiation clouds dissipating   It was a special day for some special dogs   We'll brighten up your patio, shove a couple of creepers up your trellis   This was Haiti last February No charge against the former first lady seems too extreme Nice weather, spring, it's so wonderful   Do you know the name of the astronaut who became America's first man in space   It happened today twenty-five years ago   Will the 49,000 who had to be evacuated from the area ever be able to go home again   That's something I can't give any credence to without a professional evaluation   A mother and her 13 year old son were both selling drugs   This is holocaust remembrance day   How big a ransom did the letter ask for

26

Police say he's been granted political asylum   For now the radioactive dirt stays where it is   Wild increases will not be permitted   The first tall ship arrives in New York for operation op-sail   She is wonderful, she is a symbol of freedom   They specialize in hate mongering and hysteria   I'm really impressed with the dedication of heart teams   I felt totally helpless, needy and afraid   6% of psychiatrists admit to having sex with their patients   He owns exotic real estate around the world   Bavarian hay is radioactive   The senate passed a sweeping tax reform bill   It was the idea of testifying against someone with Goth's reputation that frightened them   It was the fantasies the customers brought with them that made the clubs so popular   You grew up in Ireland   What did you think about America   Liberty is the most important thing that any person or any country can have   She's won two academy awards   I feel threatened by the responsibility of my intellect   It's perfectly all right for a child to say I hate you   I'm very skeptical when the government speaks of reform   Solidarity is wounded, many Poles say, but it is not dead   That would seem to diminish chances for a summit   Friends and family ready to attend his wedding were shocked   It just works like a miracle   Gonzalez added that due to previous corruption, this health center—Guatemala's largest—is operating under a 10 million quetzal budget deficit and that it has apportioned 72 centavos (about 27¢) to feed each in-patient each day   The judge ruled her life was so wracked with pain it would be cruel to make her go on   It also attracted migrating birds   He suggested a statue commemorating American Independence at a dinner party in France   Exciting time period, here I have a girlfriend, she's from Phoenix   Let's begin with cuts, bruises and scrapes   That's the original mold of the ear of the Statue of Liberty   Definitely a better weapon for our people   The oldest ship in the world, the Gazella, has reigned over the high seas for 103 years   You can get a Liberty plate when you reregister your car or register a new one   It came over in 213 crates   The people of Newark have heard promises before

28

The huge fire started suddenly and spread quickly   Yesterday New York's highest court reinstated the charge   She must receive constant psychiatric care while incarcerated   To put it bluntly, Mother Superior has had it   This report concludes that violent pornography leads to sexual violence   There will be no labor day parade this year   The Cyclone is finally running again after an insurance crisis shut it down   The court was, to a certain extent, sympathetic   It was the most serious attempt to infiltrate Israel in over a year   Inside are two million bitter and frustrated people   A link between stressful social environments and tobacco   Those are the folks who have an allergy to fresh fruit   You could be in shock and dead in two minutes   Taking a logo and making it huge is very 1980s pop   The laughter really rocks the theater   Whatever it is that we do easily and well is often the least interesting part of our lives   As she went through customs in Chicago, she was held two hours, and was searched and harassed by customs officials who called her a "subversive"   A main theme of the demonstration was to protest the rising cost of living and the government's new economic package   The seven person crew doesn't have the money   They say he's paralyzed from the neck down   He's armed with a gun, a small silver gun   It's a miracle that they made it   An earthquake rocks Southern California, the second time in a week   The forty-three-year-old senator overwhelmed his competition Illegal aliens are eligible for Medicaid   New Jersey ranks fourth among the fifty states in the number of AIDS cases   Most democrats like to sleep in their pajamas and make love to their husbands while republicans prefer nightgowns and watching TV   Today oil prices were on a new plunge   The lightweight, million dollar aircraft stayed aloft for almost five days   AIDS related discrimination will not be tolerated   I didn't need Bernard Goetz to promote my career   A lot of people on Manhattan's East Side think their busdrivers have gone mad

29

Anybody can go into the pay phone business   We will never stop drug availability in this country by law enforcement measures alone   We should exert that force in terms of morality   Talks will resume without any preconditions   40,000 tons of uncollected garbage   With this drug doctors can use the patient's own bone marrow   Aerobics are being presented here as a national sport   We need more hospital beds for psychiatric patients   This is an extraordinary bipartisan effort Fairness will be in the eyes of the beholder   Some businesses pay no tax at all   The pilots who will carry the Bolivians into action carry hand guns   The garbage will be picked up, starting tomorrow   The rich and famous are gathering at Cape Cod   The Hispanic World's Fair has been around for eight years   You don't allow yourself to be as open and friendly as you would like to be   You're not getting older, you're getting better   GAM leaders told Cerezo that they do not expect him to investigate the whereabouts of the 40,000 Guatemalans estimated to have disappeared during the past twenty years, but are demanding the investigation of some 850 documented cases that took place between 1980 and 1985   Black unions have already paid a heavy price Swimmers in their eighties were competing stroke by stroke   More than 500 movies have been captioned for the hearing impaired   It was a revolution in crime busting Rock 'n Roll is now Rock 'n Rap   Mrs. Abzug was in the middle of a political campaign when her husband of more than 40 years died   Making this film was like going to a party, you just sat around and created this little world   On this day in 1899 Ernest Papa Hemingway was born in a suburb of Chicago   The law just went into effect a year or so ago   Today the place was virtually wall to wall with cops   Can you inflict injury   Can you attract attention   Did you know that consumers bothered to redeem only about 4%   The drug itself seems to be winning the war   He killed the child with his bare hands   Crack had its genesis in the Bronx in 1984   Neighborhood activists continue to press their case

34

What is the plight of the Soviet Jew in general   He's been held since
Saturday, allegedly for spying   Officials are investigating the
cause of the fire   Thirty million men are bald   40% of us dream
in color   Calvin Klein has not one but two shops in Flemington, NJ
Officials think that it might have been tampered with right in
the store   He died less than three hours later   Passenger service
losses have kept it in the red for the last six years   Next
they'll have to give us money to take cars   Tests of fitness of
American youths have revealed terrible deficits   The hijackers
are believed to be Palestinian terrorists   Just a nice person
Some children in this area will never see the inside of a classroom
The hijackers boarded the plane dressed as security guards
Negotiate, negotiate, negotiate   Buy time, buy time, buy time
Overpopulation in the animal world is a problem most people ignore
Inside more than 25 men were praying   I think they're just stunned
Where were the commandos   They must come out   Her feet and face
were hit with shrapnel   A major upset at the open   Police are
now looking for those who caused his death   He thinks the Soviets
are going to try him for espionage   A formal investigation will
now be launched   The nights, he said, are cold here   In the
evening, when it's dark, I get a little paranoid   Some of the
wounded to a U. S. hospital near Frankfurt   At least five airport
guards have been suspended since the incident   There is no other
peaceful way to reform   Then the lights went out and the shooting
started   When the fellow told us to put our hands up   I have
found out the child was one of the victims   Students say they will
never forget this man of peace   Five of his bodyguards were killed
The trouble college educated women over 30 have finding a man
Truck drivers are the first advocates of raising the speed limit
Will Frank Sinatra be known as the chairman of the broads   Perry
Como began his career over 50 years ago   If I didn't do some of
those old things they'd start to yell at me   He goes to bed at
six in the morning and gets up at four in the afternoon

47

Two people are dead after a bizarre shoot-out in a street in Queens   They are willing to pay $25,000 to get him into custody   When it comes to sex what should young ears hear   Four of those arrested were army officers   There really aren't any anti-cavity foods   It would label them as handicapped citizens   What drove a fourteen year-old high school freshman to murder   Chambers claimed he killed her accidentally in rough sex play   It's a terrific way to end the year   It looks just like my own teeth the caps are porcelain and tend to last much longer   The police have surrounded a housing project   It's obvious that the execution of these policies was flawed, and mistakes were made   Anything that weakens America weakens Europe, indeed the whole of the free world   How could it have happened in the first place   Thousands of French students fighting with police and turning the streets of Paris into a battle   The house democratic leader disagreed with the President's assessment   Republican governors had reason to be jolly   Israeli troops shot and wounded a Palestinian youth   No president takes kindly to press criticism   Is the press enjoying this crisis   45 years ago today Japan attacked Pearl Harbor   Otherwise you make it too easy for thieves to attempt a forgery   It was an extraordinary setting for an extraordinary story   Shultz called the contra connection a mistake   There's less political activism on campus   The fighting near the border area has died down   Almost 1000 small fry were welcome to Macy's this morning   I wanted this the most because it lights up in the dark   We have methods to modify our treatment so you won't have any pain   Where is the benzene coming from, and who's to blame   It will be a while before anyone receives a reward for the capture of Larry Davis   I'm impressed with his ability to cut through a lot of red tape   I think I can never retire—I have to keep working   The technique of video is absolutely remarkable   He knew the navy would teach him to fly   It was a bad case of combat fatigue that forced him to quit

Edward Dorn

The Cosmology of Finding Your Spot

The *Resistantism* of all other places
On the floor among filters and the Spillings
   The cosmology of the floor of the Nation
   The cosmology of finding your place
      The cosmology of smelling and feeling your Natural place
     inside the place, feeling the filters
      feeling the rock, feeling the roll
       feeling the social spray at that level
        low down, with the filters and the feet
         feeling the place you can fold all four legs
         and be man's best friend to the End, among the filters
         and the feet, in the rock, and in the roll
       in the clock and in the roll, in the hole
      of the social bilge **The Great White Dog**
     of the Rockchalk, seeks his place Seeks
      The place for Him there, tries every scrap of Space
   The Great White Dog of The Rockchalk Cafe
   moves under the Social seeking his own Place
   in the constant present snap of eternity
   listening with the german dislocated castenet
His Nose Is under the great pin ball rolling in heaven above
  thru the barren terrain of feet He moves
from place to place seeking his place
The resisters the dogs seek their place
WAYNE KIMBALL told me all this
WAYNE KIMBALL sits in the booths, WAYNE KIMBALL
  knows about the *Great White Dog of the Rockchalk*
  The Great White Dog of The Rockchalk doesn't

The Great White Dog has been there
Western Civilization is Beer
   The Great White Dog of The Rockchalk
   went thru the door of Western Civilization
      Which is north of the Barbershop
      and north of the sailor pants incense shop
         The Great White Dog went between all that
         and the Gaslight, *The Great White Rockchalk dog*
            shakes hands with both paws indiscriminately
            For he Seeks his own true place on the floor
               He disregards the social He seeks the Place
               he seeks The Space his **soul** can occupy
                  In His restless search he looks only for the Place
                  Where he can come to rest in his own true Place
                  and that might be on the floor of the rockchalk
                  The great *White Dog* is not Interdicted by opinion
                  He accepts the floor of the *Rock Chalk* as an Area,
                  like any other, he will test that space
               He is preoccupied only with the Search
               The Great White dog of the Rockchalk is not social
               WAYNE KIMBALL told me all this, WAYNE KIMBALL
            is social, he knows only persons, he doesn't
         give a shit for the floor of the *Rockchalk*
            WAYNE KIMBALL is neurotic like us, he wants
         to smoke Grass, WAYNE KIMBALL sits in the booths
         WAYNE KIMBALL drinks beer, has a part time job
      pretending to be literate, WAYNE KIMBALL uses
      the telephone and all other public Utilities
including Cocaine, *The Great White Dog*
of the Rock Chalk is full of shit and can't shit
until he finds his place, WAYNE KIMBALL has diarrhea
WAYNE KIMBALL hasn't got a driver's license
   WAYNE KIMBALL is thin and knows everything that happens
      He has ears, He is a corrupt little mongrel like us
         turned on to everything hopeless and bullsIiit

The Great White Dog of The Rockchalk is dumb
    and doesn't know anything but his instinct for the search
  for his place somewhere in the litter
    of the filters and tile literally dropped dreams
    of the *Great Rock Chalk*, he smells the dreams
      on the floor dropped from between the legs
      of young English majors, ejected from between the
        Dual Spraycans of the fraternizers
        He seeks his place on top of this matter
          among tile feet of the privileged nation on the floor
          of the Great shit, Rock Chalk Rock Chalk White Rock
          Chalk Dog, And WAYNE KIMBALL Smokes cigarettes
          and Thoreaus them ontoOntoOntoOnto the floor
        already predicated by cancer, the slow movement of *Cancer*
        and I love these dogs because they are us and more us
      than we are and they seek their places as do the true
      whether they are *Resisters* or just scared or both
      They are the twin dogs of creation in our image
      and I give them both the floor as I give the *Resisters*
     This Poem from the throne of Belief as the **Egyptians**
     Gave and took from the Dogs Their access to Heaven
    That we may all be Gods and seek our Place.

(Presented April 10, 1969, at the United Campus Christian Fellowship Benefit Reading for the Draft Resister League, Lawrence)

On the Edge of the Badlands

There is a regular stop out here
named Cactus Flat
where this incorporated ear
was nailed like Ulysses
to the side of a police dog

Mesozoic Landscape

Mesozoic Landscape

> Anything that looks like
> A Solution
> is as ridiculous as the Problem
>
> ?

He read the *Coca leaves* three times
Each time they told him . .

        Cascades of) **HAND JIVE**

SOCIAL CONTROL ⟶ ⎱ the unit
                                    ⎰ Someone hiding all over the unit
                                    an idea has been bouncing around
                                        the unit in the past few hours
                                  she let go and sprayed all over the unit

                                          (27 yr old athlete
                              E) eleville (mood elevators))   admitted (to the
                                like a towne in Kansas   Unit) six mos ago
                                                            "upset because
                                                                he is getting old'

"of course this is all reviled
but then, thats the rush
      And they reviled him entire
when they extracted the five o'clock shadow
in 1960 before the pepsi episode

                                                   a major invasion
                                                       of the modality

        episodic lunacy

                                          Electric treatment
                         an electospasmodic smile graced
                       his lips,
                               as he faced the crowd
                                   . . . **lowd**

                     mensural

The Turk

Leading off with a statement
like "I am Jesus Christ,"
was perhaps a bit strong.
Nevertheless, if Jesus Christ
were to return to Earth,
He'd shoot the Pope.

                              A "found" abhorrence
                              1 April 1985

■

"Why is wanting to kill Ronald Reagan
and Fuck Jody Foster
considered insane?
Makes no sense to me."

                              (from 2nd floor toilet
                              Hellems, U. C. Boulder,
                              by a philosophy student
                              I would imagine.)

Kenward Elmslie

Sin in the Hinterlands

      'Grashulations, Fingerprint Man!
Then rush rush, slip off white covers, simple home ceremony,
      foto, foto-rinse, foto-bins.

      Then home. Climb into padded think trunk,
wait for burble of ancestry info: bio. Canned info bio. Canned
      bio logo with Daffy Duck forefinger blur:

      told you so (spinster) told you so.
No foxtrot, luxury of foxtrot, foxtrot dip, dip gimp of Valhalla.
      Dick fun tone of voice

      stalled between floors.
Sick sun screened by healthy fog, uniform as skeeter netting.
      Afterlife of tone of voice.

      Ectoplasm abandonment:
raggedy edges sneaking out on us soundlessly: left to stare at soup
      in valley bowl, remote milk soup.

      A simon-pure energy vestige, kaput.
Get it? Another solid blue day of role reversals, healthy sun,
      sick wisp kaput, as in sex act cordoned off

      in the silliness of a reflecting pool.
Malarial feel about things, people in charge long since gone.
      Kind of stamina outpost life thrives on.

Lip-sync, a life of lip-sync,
it's like a life of lip-sync, lip-sync of tip of vat, hot vat.
Inner rush of believability upsurge.

Juicier colors and whoppers.
Automatic side—effect: beautification apex with skeered frills—
mound of black tires at end of track.

To help maintenance of upsurge,
tree, an up, bluejay squawks, nubbin doodads, tree turning
upside down.
Imbedded birds. Dormant cornucopia: freeze it.

Ron Dossier

pre-natal barreling through flatness
into a red dawn
geared to mime
of silent scream

      trompe l'oeil oilscape
      of roadrunners in Baby Snooks snoods
      hustling up and down derricks
      facing zilch decisive moments
      breaking all hokum records
      in Souseland,
      a.k.a Mouseland,
      of polkadot jumpsuits (blurry)

paroxysms of holy shit hilarity
at the mounds of vaseline
shimmering with high-zonk rainbows
and (huge AND)
orange fright wigs askew
on the obligatory long horn skulls

      Ice Age overview
      somewhat in the canned laughter
      of the air conditioned iguana brain:
      pablum of smoke signals
      creates found object
      that'll never get lost,
      sawn in two-o-o-o-o,
      guts plopped out
      tap cheroot
      all tuned up
      ready to go

      same old
       day old
       coolth

Hand

The hand, wizened but sprightly, circled the round toolshed, hunting for Romulus and Remus in what it took to be the total chaos of Outer Space. The dissonance that sounded like time moving backward faster and faster was actually the racket some pals of the Dawn Brigade (out scrounging for circuits) were making, hurling hard balls of mica at zombies (this is what's so ironic)—victims of amnesia (this is what's so ironic)—but elephant-sized standing in the endless swamp.

Nytol

From Saga of Skunk's Misery

Gomer Pyle chipmunk
chomps up ... it's Carol Burnett
held 'tween paws like ice cream cone.

Strobe lit wit lobe deranged.
Balding babies speed up the re-runs.
    Grasshopper!
    Grasshopper!
    Grasshopper!

from Cyberspace

Jibber-jabber about my new browser,
ground-level know-how, her groupie
thang. Sod babe exclusivity. Pick up
Nazi Nite Smile muff, white angora
bobbysox. Neo Puppylove Retro-30s.

Peter Orlovsky

Lines of Feeling

The mountain bear has a hole in his pants—trouble
Doctors get free passes to my museum
in return for there labatomies on me
I am not afraid to work—I would love to fly a dirigible.
Nor am I afraid to be a colector of lamps—
provided everyone help me.
And as for your cantelopes, 2/29—I consider it dangerous.
My fortune is dedicated to the movies.
I dont go out anywhare without my belt
cause I own everything that lays inside my belt
And when ever thers a man on the corner
Telling me theres a boat leaving for heaven now
I'll go & never speek another word.
Piano played with tears. Its so easy to jerk off!
Look mister will you give me a pair of pajamers.

There was this fellow I was telling you about
who built something in his room, he built & built
untill it got to big for his room, then he had to move,
then he always had to move, that was him.
Then this new fellow who went out to the store
& he walked & he walked, and one block went behind him,
& so on till he was far away from home—
all because of the way someone said
something on T.V.

O science give me twenty feet
twenty grandma meet ball eyes
take me apart in the robot room
do me up right
just give me one thing extraordinary
(I got something going here now
dont rush me, I got this typewritter, right
got this paper here right
all alone, right—)
How much beauty has rolled off the breast of a dying swan?

1963 San Francisco

Ted Berrigan

Ass-face

"This is the only language you understand, Ass-Face!"

Rochelle Owens

Not Be Essence That Cannot Be

    Yields
(Which see)
        Azzas
See which
Picker-tool
Azzas
Wielding
A a growing
Iso-
Lation

Two
That for
Spec-
Ial sperm
Prodigal horse
Spechez
Luminus
Which after
Die. Nine (nin)
Twists made in
Voles water-
Ing
Juicy.

Belonged into Sheepshank

Hunger
It is luck too. Hullabaloo Vishnu
Knowledge birds liturgic liverwort dynamite ne-not
Hideous Munt Jak
Barbarous.
Rosy.
Like emblem on the teeth. Two, the best
I pray thee, the nose leaking, the indians, the words
And songs
Nimble feeted.
Enlightened
Be a cold
Thing.
The same time. Tied to no place
Belonged into Sheepshank punjabi delusion
Unreal with no
Thing.
Lived.
Which my Pope. Bent over
Made pregnant ordained bursted the good
Fat foreskin
Sighed.
After entombment
And carpfishes.
Tonkin
Mere not Simon Magus. He was emptied
Before the man and animal mentally again and again
Between the hole of the mouth
And ass hole.
The base salty.
Some matter. I emit
I hold value and attached butter-fat love
Good selfishness
Burnt clay.
Unclearly christian
For a hump.

Zu Zu Midday I'm Narcotic

Endlong skirmish lump
I am gallant, greek
Nightingale, zu zu
Midday I'm narcotic,
Light, ball-flowered
Fly, ku ku ven-emous
Beyond wood luring
Stick, polled, over

My mucous, meaning
Many me's hot-short
Poor snakemouth I
Sence eels sneering
My forward voo doo
To and fro, seven
puffs, to and fro
ME, white-colored

YOU muck luck dope
A evil drink, top
Of a wapiti poyo,
YOU goo me bloodshot
YOU whacky fop, O Oph
Elia you milk the
Pocket-knife poko
On holidays in the sun

Tom Raworth

Wandergut

From *The Hungarian*

slovak intellectual appears to cyclops
resembling your face
hiding ecstasy in cement works of webern
cutlass banana-scar on amber mind-nuts

oval, a robot tu-tu
lovingly spins metalically among the tortoises
with seventeen sporadic rotors
similarly steaming egyptian musaz

pieter kelnek who in moderation
seemed the energy of spinning sarcasm
semi-exerted
takes from it a slovak intellectual

Sally to See You, Tacitus

amok among sicilians
seeking far with my good eye
can alcohol
so maintain europe
that the gone rue it so?

is it a first-greeting fist then
that sparks on nearing
a merry parent?
is this the foolish cyclamate
ten gallons of which flatten your hair?

exercise that lengthens dogs
mars their true coats
"holy mitred vale
of tulsa pray for us"
yes lola.... no giorgio.... hi joe

At Maximum Zero

seeking the still window
in stasis
a variant arrival
chortles into a hold-all
golden arrival-window!

lo! nears the orgone-bug
—mincy ugly tunneler—
each distant foot feels all
eggy   agony in a homosexual's apartment
eggy future in a blimp sack

"ballast" (ricardo montalban)
a fat lip
leapfrogging
hold! ho! lobster's
name instructs the eggy cherub

How Cold Is Most

how easy to hold fania's hat
a muscled yogi will hold it
this visitor to our ranks
will hold it vaguely
go hunting with fania

loan your writ or go in a bug
mind the ugly will
allegro!   feldspar!
behold the clear painful beauty of your tie
behold saki futilely inflate you

"by allah!"—from a valise
a quick fist
an opal yak
old   o.... bangkok
fate is far from syrup's ego

Clark Coolidge

"HEY! YOU LOOK LIKE A GIRL"

the "Erector Sets" were permanent they thought, & forgot & left
    the bridges up
wheel zimmer kids all over ("America's Famous Rivers") & the country
    might tilt, toward you, up dangerously
Look out! Fire Pa by the House Kite! & the Lemon o' the Lake freaks
    humid ventilators & mates quail-fish

O, let's snout & lunge, baste & hasten Popeye! (he came over
    in a brick faceted tractor glare) the Three Kneeless
        Brothers! o bejeweled terraced rims of Hoke & "morn"!
the limits of New Jersey have been legally equated with the
    limbs of tobacco   & Jimmy's wand
        wrecked his bridge-pool mother (a "family of 5 . . .")

a kind of Lockjaw discovered in snails only under
    cement & steel abutment bridges? guess so.
what, a tropical fungul-film of green pin fish? Geeks
    authored Biblical Humor at bloody stumps! Yes!
& milk flange ups Vitamin C , & babies' mildew sold
    a solid gleam on carpets, & the mysterious black gland
(doctors hid it) found to provide 98% champion gliders of kites

the transparent mantids rest on highest knit girders for their nests, tho
    the belted cops have vacated Colorado forever
Chipmunk Berries kept the "war effort" hung in bulge
    & fire creeps to cement the mothers flee! (Buy a Kit!)
        Bee grew a beard! won a prize!

Cracker jacks emit "a weird light"
N.Y.Times legends' flutters ooze crabs below Hudson's "Green" Level
Calcomine gives the air to ceilings & mush
   tone California "level housing," sounding like neon, crushed
     (road-like) into the landing sea

too loud! move that Grape, the beds too lavender, & lounge "<u>is too!</u>"
   I couldn't believe either in the "car park" (at all)
     specially when you untied & left
       your raspberry ribbon that snaps
         & all & that too - "so true!"

toads in the mumble park "levels" humming by
ooooof! your lunch, I'd unlock my hand if I
   were wearing a glove. Love's definitely <u>round!</u>

& nothing has been recently found to be
    forever.

Acid

Blackie was met at the subway
advertising
wished for pumice sunny flags
WE GO   DOWN WE   GO DOWN

"Giant Grouper" said, in cold spray net tank
        GREENS deep at me
fade corridors
tapped the wrong uncle & spoke intimately

in foetal lift of potty stalagmites, resting
hair pillows edges of dead batteries
the leak
        Growth Mustard

earth   vanity error: drainage , settle
        cigarette balls on umber pools
           the corners left to never return . . .

"call soon, I was underground"

Fed Drapes

FELL FAR BUT THE BARN (came) up & smacked me
Who're you, bleedin? Fled.
Blat in back of a Victrola Car
is so red is such that sun
fell in the rushes & pen bear appear

the white wrong numeral on the wall
can't take it off with the clock
       down with the clock it . . .
          way
on the board-couch with brass, kindergarten clench joints
backed violet rip into the gas valve
it hemmed & snowed

      the wrong way
        remnant face
         rubber
      the pucker

Crisp Loss

red eggless drop-closet days
too angle-tuned to be numb
his leg... no, smileless   glass eels
fall-out into the silt lesson, cab-edges
roughen the skin around the lapel, the lemon
hedges & widens, pulling in the direct forcep: the laughter

red-lead window of classic farm marshes
eeking in the snub of oil, & tanned sandwiches
roughage at the elbow, but clear neon ahead   step
up tuba & buckle don't wait around the rims
his vents of the hum passage... no.

eggs on sleeve visions of the pyrite mine, Amen.

yellow days thudding to battery-park.   elms
spreading bacilli & wires, mind drone, cheese melting
lucky rims, in back of the mobile palace,   fleet
turnover in smiler mushrooms, beaks fading
tower of lice & the flag next house, "what ditch?"
"Marry me" & cheese-graters & the sons of the pioneers

black pits, how can the flame be sunk?

      toe neons & toe neons

Machinations Calcite

Acetone imprinted
oblique swatch on the skin car barn oil wall
ocarina & mumps
much wet green
I'd leave sole key to this game to my friend, sheet water cat.

actor impressed
weaving candle turn on computer cigarette, paper wall
tarheels & balance
a lot of yellow stick neck
He'll have to hurry & carry away, to my blue friend hustling bringing
                                              his moon & car

Agate inked
merry melodies drool on shank of wet lead star tool
crayon & sand
length of granite buck-drill
It's sucking up the strand, his crystal flag, & the eels tube for that,
                                              their parade swizzle fun

arctic suck
splinter dry ice spazz luke-ing ace supper at church
hard pinks & sponge breath
many forearms drift
Roller window going up on I repeat my offer food list in iron flakes

The Automatic Nerve at Razed Heights

From *On the Nameways*

Sure thing Philip Morris is up your ass
and the brinks of it all grow lazy
machined endings of gloss and relapse
just the tug to get it towed

Seems she has to take a snake
to the doctor as his time seemed up
but who's to know as the plant
blows out and there's a possible cease
to the accompanying freaky green chorus

Time to take up something practical
like your pants in a row
those tones in the ditch your everloving
kamikaze lesson-bearing toot-boy
gone as Chewbacca and just as
how-do-you-want-your

Pumper Mouth

Small analgesic membrane tocsins
one foot on the shore
we'll have to go home now Brainy
the capes no longer open
to such frosty fools
neatscap and the lob
now go
pull all the yell ropes on Popeye's math

Gulp

Do you see that building behind us?
the tiny inhabitants land on actual brains
all the very hands have been wiped away
Doctor Mooncell here higher than any window
but three boners later
the meaninglessness of clothing in the face of
too many beings dreaming of the sun wind
the nuts and bolts of battle
all in a book titled Granite in Toto
Edward Dahlberg banished beyond Pluto
"just get over it, sweaterhead"
do these dolphins want the baloney to arrive?
recalcitrance the key to connectivity
you turn over and over in your sleep
a shakiness of the tonal hemispheres
but is this the way to probe death?
candied lights in long dark rooms?
code name Bladder Tribes
now there's a new use for all these worlds
let the Gummy Bears bear me
out

Jim Brodey

Bum Trip

Garlic, strong & fresh, French licorice
musk-lathered & vain, inter-
uterine freaks fistfucking numb pork,
mucilage oily on the deep fry,
flesh stripped away to expose the grace
as a beard piping hot to elephants
with onion rings for eyes, smashed pearls,
nobody listening, one big superlative yawn
separate & divine as a gibbering goy in hock,
"and our driver's face is always
well hidden," smiling as the cat shit
lands on your face & rolls into your Bloody Mary
then downshifts roaring out of a head in flames,
reticent before the most scrumptious eagles
piss Gatorade into bulletholes, serenity
blushed like a sun in nova, what
comes over you emptying your being
to a thirst for vomit in the wind

Anne Tardos

from Ginkgo Knuckle Nubia

Penguin hubbub Jesus worship
Pyramidal mudpack
Daddy-longlegs cemetery

Dodo.

Penguin hubbub Jesus worship is the actual hubbub heard among penguins who have congregated in order to worship Jesus.

A daddy-longlegs cemetery is usually a matchbox of some sort.

Poodle viceroy salad dressing
Nympholeptic sitzbath
Mummified cadenza friction

Erotica.

Poodle viceroy salad dressing refers to a poodle who not only made it to viceroyhood, but who has since developed a taste for salad dressing.

from Considerations

Morphological nitpicking venue
Rabbit hole vegetarian menu
Nimbus glory
Pokerfaced bunny mummy
And the loudest radio galaxy *I* ever knew

Bunny mummies have been spotted near radio galaxies. Scientists fail to understand the significance of this phenomenon. Their faces are expressionless and there appears to be a nimbus around their heads. The bunnies,' not the scientists.'

Academic battlement flickering
Boxturtle blazer dyke's bickering
Bauhaus functionalism
Intramural individualism
Laughable latitude lingering

Boxturtles who enjoy bickering with lesbians are usually fervent proponents of the functionality of Bauhaus

Quintuplicated cardigan
Wrapped around a ptarmigan
Monorail rattlesnake
Rabble-rouser drink take
Danced around the room again

Ptarmigans have a tendency to feel cold and often need five or six cardigans to get warm. Rattlesnakes love riding the monorail.

Aram Saroyan

oh oh oh oh oh oh oh oh oh

suggest bear

oh oh oh oh oh oh oh oh oh

Bernadette Mayer

On Barnard

Send me the tone that sings
"Cockroaches in your ass
and a flying ride home."
Is there a cure for elephantiasis
And if not why fabricate
the breeches that will
keep us in our cocks.
A couch is but an imprimatur
for farts.
And candles and flaming
irons light the purple
caves of dripping maturity.
Put on your cloaks and
daggers will assume the
places of slaves.
In the quivering
equivalency of lengths
of hairs and days
the woman will be the boys.

François Villon Follows the Thin Lion

For Bill Berkson

                fill the tin voodoos
Ovid's dill moon, the doffers hunt
to loop.
doll-less in linnets.
Dillon pilfers oolfoos, fin-lips!
                the thinning third
                      of avoir dupois.
Huns unlid at the onicker's kiln
      a flint and a linx,
      the infinite minnow.
off lighting
fools lift digits
the lieutenant fills the ocean
                    give him onions.

Thick

Hashish the Ghost is rumored dead
       the slow boor had the rheum
       worm and bug gagging him
       higher than a gourd shouting whoosh
a shower and the rum you piggish shrew
to oust your mother from the same shroud as you

Owl, bitch, hog and whore met at the bogs' mouth
                       to bludgeon the womb

      it was only a gag
      at least the author's brought his luger
      he's ogling that myth

a gob of rum for the wretch with the hookah
              the oil-rout grew
              bulging the gulch with rush & shout
              there boils the ocean.

We've Solved the Problem

we've solved the problem, the problem is solved

    men are women, women are men

        i'm pregnant for a while, you're

pregnant for a while

    "if someone doesn't change into an animal,

        we won't be saved"   someone must

change into an animal so that we can be saved.

        a man turns into a cat

          a man becomes a cat

he gives himself to his friends in the form

        of lead & coal

the man-cat gives himself to us in the

        form of lead & coal

he draws himself

    with lead & coal, the lead & coal man-cat

draws a picture of himself

      he is a girl

    the man is a girl—in black & white,

she sings

      there are brush fires burning

A Catskill Eagle

Not a song of love but
When I ask George
Does he have a handgun
He says, "Sure Baby"

Otherwise it's dark
Why don't you drive & arrive up here
In your reversing Lochinvarish Chrysler Reliant
I've got my period & bleed in my Plymouth Horizon
Like when we went to the cave in your Volkswagen bus

O dear Sir Lancelot
Would you want this particular bowl?
Poor Arthur it is not his cock
The search being over of some mystery

I put something wooden in my mouth and on the safe porch
    I fear the absences of friends who were once here
    sitting laughing at this table, a rectangle, they
    were driving a Renault Le Car

Steve McCaffery

from Teachable Texts

It's suffocation time again
how's that for temperature
as if your shit could think
chiasmus without consequences
herring bone at brink of
tide pool education
a composed puss in my boots

memory deserves the best
like the time it all happened for once
without stetch-book momentum
demarcation reached by
Bloop street serenade then
digitally remastered   sounds of
Pol Pot from the dugout
posse dress   magenta sweaters
holding swab safely thinks
i'm not Picasso.   *i'm* out of breath
thinks again
metaphysics of presence is not an innocence
it's pancakes like the rest of
yesterday's support of sense except this year
it began with the drapes and the cleaning bill

body skid without entering the ear canal
the logicells clearing on instant contact
showbizz retina and all that snore tactics
white's utter tournament time
back to the sea is it?
or probably should be
seepage via a split screen anamnesis

reconnected from
its background grunt of scalpels.

as death so life
my dixie cup within whisper range
its violet voice the particles of raccoon smashed
and the hyssop
dominant through perfected summer rains
or was it a crevice made for taxis?
(crude bark logic) (wanton flops taxonomy)
to starboard and i'm not even sailing.)
become a copper
flush the junkies out from a used suitcase
to gorsefileds somewhat east
of turning dark

vomiting on Burns' night
elemental chill with linebreak
check out this holograph
it's either light or charcoal
dinks a dawn hardly
racist slang to the myrrh-fudge
sucked sideways into sports.

so are we getting happier?
my style of impotence dilutes
then depoliticizes
says hello then shuts up
thermometer repeating drinks in moderation
alcohol compared to tracksuits
the crotch is the first to go
thread by thread with the zipper side up
where your smile says goodbye
then i'm leaving.

Canada counts its transhistoric debt
in the text that Sarah mentions.
Questions three: what's Sarah
perhaps the most famous infinite of all

Bob Perelman

PICTURE

Picture (see, control, dominate) a
Phallocentric lawyer dominating a Snickers, Milky Way, or Mars Bar
On Market Street in the spermy light
Of day. "I couldn't care less"

I'm not going to get off his case
Until the subject, a 10 foot tall ogre
Sulking at the conference table, changes nature.
Unknowable, domineering, ravening, question-begging, life-
Destroying, tune-mongering calliope. Always
At a moment's notice, water's edge, eye
Hems its own parade, sinks into past. You can't believe
What you read. "I wouldn't if I were you"

For only in this way can the poem
Be returned to the mind (a mouth).
A man's large, erect penis and a woman's
Larger, more erect penis, these are the strategic materials

For the in-touch scenarios of people
Who husband the earth's increasingly scarce
Strategic materials. The mighty engine
Mounts the throne, of egg and semen made.

DON'T DRINK THE WATER, EAT THE FOOD, OR BREATHE THE AIR

My perfect life is being spoiled
By this shitty army food. Radioactive
Waters in the salad dressing are discoloring
My perfect pornographic page (the real thing),

Its thighs geometric, meretricious.
Torn-up grandmothers in El Salvador
My beautiful sky don't touch me or it'll go partly cloudy.
Envelope-language means nothing. Tear it open.

A number of other lives. Tears, cheers, applications.
So now you have a perfect one inch vegetable word generator in my
    head.
It thinks. Stupid baby grown up extremely accurate.
Lob the applause meter right into the mens room at the Kremlin.

It is perfectly reasonable to be so annoyed
With the lack of respect one receives from the media
(Institutional acronyms spread putative paper legs
To a trillion dollar wind) that one thinks

Of the five hundred thousand dead communists
In Indonesia as sick caribou
Culled from the herd by the skilled PBS wolves.
This thin tundra snow makes a perfect backdrop.

MENTAL IMAGERY

My grandmother grew up on a farm
Somewhere in my mind. Estonia, I think.
There were no people there, only me.
Where once were vaginas like Bibles
And penises like bookmarks, now groups

Of chemically hounded hunters and gatherers
Huddle around the TV, a combination
Digestative and glory hole, glowing
In a permanent rightwing fundraiser
(The structuralist stunned in the tub,
The tide of signifiers (resumés) rising).

Now there is nothing wrong with having
A baby, though a few strategic needs might place
Childcare on the back burner. Somebody
Wants nobody in particular's oil. I want everybody
To talk. Tumultuous applause. I want everybody
(Letters literally burned into wood) to be home.
Unclean thoughts attach to counted bodies.

Here I am, man's clothes on a woman's baby.
The brain is a reducing valve, one
That doesn't work, watch. This salt shaker
(My features, irreducible)
Won't leave here without me.

UP MEMORY LANE

Give yourself one point for each time sense data mount
Up and suck you through the window. These
Single things left over from dream ovens.
Water makes a pretty picture.

date 2nd the on woman the of image sleep the said you love I
water aren't people. pore every from love Radiating

Why am I doing this?
Asks Dobie Gillis, performing (imagine André Previn
Conducting Brahms on TV) cunnilingus on Annette Funicello
(You'll hear from my phallocentric lawyer).

Because you want to,
Need to literally like your own other.

life of facts the smear Words
desired you If. air real Through
weighed body your if, equally word Each
matter wouldn't direction then thought your as much As

But I've made my mind a land populated
way this in only for sound demons relations By
Can the poem enter the mind without
stopped effectively being and itself Disguising

SCAPEGOAT

Scraps of dogs in head, bacon. A big metal
Think tank cracks a smile, rolling down
Windows to shop the day away
To restore order. Walls call collect.
Spectators identify with the special effects

(Hear them barking?) as a beautiful industrialized
Woman, one in a million, rolls down her
Secret and drives over to your ad. My hands
(Welcome to the human race) are indefinably far
From my body. Rocky punches insurgent meat.
He'll lose. The withered plot thickens away.

Bitches of the World, unite, untie!
Male Presences, change your own diapers for a change?
Public buildings every ten blocks or so, solar, no doors!
A Poets Theater in every town!
Equip the stages with trampolines, but no P.A. systems,
No clocks, no extraterrestrial clues to meaning.

Back, earthling, to your partially eaten
Language tamer. Would you buy a used concept
From yourself? Then speak. A sentence (Here
We go again) whips itself into a frenzy of obvious
Obliterated social life. It's hazy & cool today.
The subject emerges from the rubble, ribbon,
Having survived, socially, partially eaten.

Kathy Acker

Hello, I'm Erica Jong

Hello, I'm Erica Jong. All of you liked my novel *Fear of Flying* because in it you met real people. People who loved and suffered and lived. My novel contained real people that's why you liked it. My new novel *How to Die Successfully* contains those same characters. And it contains two new characters. You and me. All of us are real. Goodbye.

Hello, I'm Erica Jong. I'm a real novelist. I write books talk to you about the agony of American life, how we all suffer, the growing pain that more and more of us are going to feel. Life in this country is going to be more horrible, unbearable, making us maniacs cause mania and death will be the only doors out of prison except for those few rich people and even they are agonized prisoners in their masks, the paths, the ways they have to act to remain who they are. You think booze sex coke rich food etc. are doors out? Temporary oblivion at best. We need total oblivion. What was I saying? Oh, yes, my name is Erica Jong

I would rather be a baby than have sex. I would rather go GOOGOO. I would write googoo. I would write

FUCK YOU UP YOUR CUNTS THAT'S WHO I AM THE FUCK WITH YOUR MONEY I'M NOT CATERING TO YOU ANYMORE I'M GETTING OUT I'M GETTING OUT I'M RIPPING UP MY CLOTHES I'M RIPPING UP MY SKIN I HURT PAIN OH HURT ME PAIN AT THIS POINT IS GOOD DO YOU UNDERSTAND? PAIN AT THIS POINT IS GOOD. ME ERICA JONG WHEE WOO WOO

I am Erica Jong I am Erica Jong fuck me you creep who's going to Australia you're leaving me all alone you're leaving me without sex I've gotten hooked on sex and now I'm

My name is Erica Jong. If there is God, God is disjunction and madness.

Yours truly, Erica Jong

Bruce Andrews

A small bird
invites all the
animals to a
great feast   Then
he pulls mountain
goats and fat out
of his rectum with
a hook and feeds
them all.   Raven
boasts, "I can do
the same."

*

They claimed that
where the hole is
is where the serial
number should
have been

Eagles Ate My Estrogen

Eagles ate my estrogen
Serum party
Scalped the jerk's hump
Dead woman kept alive to save fetus
Farmer gives birth to his pail
There *is* a tooth fairy
You either want to fuck it (?) or drain it (?)
Cargo cult begins at home
Cool the tool
Think of life in America as a kind of minimum security prison
I fault the fuck
I wept openly at the political triumph of the bourgeoisie
Cheese repents what it has done
Penis enlargement: how to make it bigger and better
Dead government kept alive to save fetus
Will the patriarchy never die?
I want batteries in bed
Curb your mom
Tampax ice cream
The husbands sleep like dogs on the floor and do all the housework
Women were always the plantation
Give up your vows
Having kids makes women stupid
Yeah man, I'm chick and you're dick
Darling you're not sperming me on
Fuck him, fuck them, & fuck you
Take your rubbers around town
Everything you know is mediocre
Women do not gain credibility when they get older—therefore, society is fucked
Mommy, I can't turn off the garbage disposal!
Big cricket ejaculated under my bed!
Just because Alan Alda is a feminist doesn't mean he's interesting.

Every mother's son dips his little weenie into the ink
Trade your baby for a car
Temporary clitorectomy
Teen kills mother to get family car
Hey, sexy bloodbath
'Hi, nice to meet you. Can I die in your tunnel?'
Big hypodermics of structural marxism, *stick it to them*
Can't I say cunt when I don't have any ice?
A strategy to engage the puppet
Magic mud to get your spouse in shape
Let's go rip our orifices in public
Mugger stole my diaphragm
May all of your babies be in bottles

from Divestiture-A

'Oh, it all.' Hopefully, though, I can maintain my *views* & just not "cathect" them with very much libidinal energy, hurt, loss, etc. & the sad premonitions, liberation, counter-socialization, when that meant contention, out in the back yard watering his flag. Milk tends to symbolize security. Clamps pulpit jackals—'Are you sure I'm breathing'—soothes sewn sky chart gossip, i.e., if hierarchical situations are *rejected* by men.... You can lick my Ramses pack. Emptying my ash trays into a parcel to send out to companies that send me junk mail with convenient business reply envelopes waiting to be filled with ash tray debris. Could you say 'Florida's legislature'—or should biological / temperamental differences be stamped out? New skepticism is not able to support the weight of the average breast. I thank you, my legs thank you; they're loading cargo at the bottom of the hour glass. You're Size 24 1/2 and You Can't Wear Pantsuits... WHO SAYS? INVENTOR Paul Davis with plastic heart built in home workshop. ALL POINTS BULLETIN. "The story must exist in each word or it cannot go on." Hero shovel, self-hanging cord attached. If nothing happened it didn't happen. Achievement is its own reward.

The average American voter—a 47 year-old wife of a machinist living in the suburbs of Dayton, Ohio. Miracle Comb Ends Gray Hair—26 Ladies in their 70s and 80s Knit Lap Robes for Paralyzed Vietnam Veterans. U. S. is Sending Arlene Dahl to Russia to Teach Women to Use Makeup. Calling the dispenser the 'honey dripper,' one could live on appeals / applause alone. "There's grape crippy crap in there"—Susan Kiehne, 12:51 a.m. "There *is* grape crippy crap in there"—Jim Kiehne, 12:59 a.m. Or merely a stick with which to flog dead dogs like Pareto. SHE RAISED MORE THAN EYEBROWS!! Leave her to limbs—indeed, just the reverse. Lobes or anxious prose in a mirror mere size frills cent kid his coat never had paper live blur red took coat saddle monkey Miss Maps. Grip. Buzz. Do microscopes turn you on? My desire for freedom is too weak, just kiss yourself and watch the blood run out, making her feel guilty, externalizing my self-dislike & laying it on her—pretty great! "What we *need* is a female victim of sudden death. Can you do it?"—you wear it when the novelty wears off BEFORE THE EVENT.

Hips protect the unborn loss of an ideal mental state. Quiet now so so much easier to memorize the present tense. Along that arch of your neck, not voluptuousness of self-doubt or self-recrimination finding a place in jerry-built life for whatever feelings. I'm blanking myself, I'm going to have a house spirited misanthropy. SELF TONES UNITE TUNING TONGUES. Hedgehogs like totalitarian worlds. [PRESENTATION—Another important criticism of Referee 3 concerns presentation (and here Referee 2 disagrees, as does Referee 1, who acknowledged that we write clearly). He states in Paragraph 1 that "simple points are made hard to grasp, presumably to give one the impression of subtle thought or to cover up dubious jumps in the logic of the article by verbal perfume." A cursory reading of our text indicates that this is *ridiculous invective*. (As for his examples, the term "self-referring" relates to an argument presented in one of the *previous works* and is clearly stated. The term "intractable"—we assumed was EASILY graspable by even the most superficial reader, etc.)] A self-basting turkey. Yet clearly the capitalist class will give up democratic forms before they will commit class suicide. I spent six years fighting Hitler for this?

Charles Bernstein

Soapy Water

You've got to be patient sometimes—sounds like an
anaesthetic, I'll be the doctor—but jump up
into the next available hoop—Nick calling
"Where are my galleys" they can't be lost
in the mail because they went Federal Express.
But something is always not there & if it's
not apparent ingenuity (the mind's perennial
ingenue) will think of it, rest enskewered.
These are the saltine days—salty & soggy. The
struts are finished, the shocks are leaking, &
like the man says, there's always a simple solution—
simple & stupid. With the rug pulled out turns
out there was no floor. & float, flutteringly
behind or in bed with what salience has no
surety. *The thing expressed*—sounds like some sort of
pizza franchise, especially with the choices
now offered—broccoli, zucchini, Belgian sausage,
seven variety mushroom. No grade like the grade
that blew the gasket. Turns out to be
slop corridor, 7 days to shapelier nail filings,
was there sex before Catholicism?
It's not as if an economy of loss is not in—
you can't say circulation because it is kind
of anticirculation: all this nervous
energy dissipates production & erodes accumulation—

so you don't have to get so dramatic, talk
about death & sex, or so moral, talk about idled
hours—all that you ever need to lose is wasting away in
anxiety's natural spring geysers. So let's
bury that knife, & in the morning we can
eat meat again.

Claire-in-the-Building

There is not a man alive who does not
admire soup. I felt that way myself
sometimes, in a manner that greatly
resembles a plug. Swerving when
there were no curbs, vying
nonchalantly against the slot-machine
logic of my temporary guardians,
dressed always in damp
patterns with inadequate pixelation
to allow for the elan she
protested she provoked on such
sleep-induced outings in partial
compliance with the work-release program
offered as an principled advance on
my prostate subjection to
tales altogether too astonishing to
submit to the usual mumbo
jumbo, you know, over easy,
eat and run, not too loud, no
bright floral patterns if
you expect to get a job in such
an incendiary application of
denouement. My word! Ellen,
did you understand one thing
Frank just said, I mean, the
nerve of these Protestants, or
whatever they call themselves
or I ain't your mother's
macaroni and cheese, please, no
ice. Is sand biodegradable?
Do you serve saws with your steak,
or are you too scared to claim
anything? *No can't do.* "I
learned to read by watching
Wheel of Fortune when I was

a baby." By the time I was 5
you couldn't tell the slippers
from the geese. That's right,
go another half mile up the cliff
and take a sharp left immediately
after where the ABSOLUTELY NO
TRESPASSING sign used to be,
you know, before the war.
Like the one about the chicken
crossed the street because he
wanted to see time fly or because
he missed the road or he didn't
want to wake up the sleeping caplets.
A very mixed-up hen. "No, I can't,
I never learned." By the time
you get up it's time to
go to sleep. Like the one about
the leaky boat and the sea's
false bottoms. Veils that part to
darker veils. So that the fissure
twisted in the vortex. Certain she was
lurking just behind the facade,
ready to explain that the joke had been
misapplied or was it, forfeited?
Never again; & again, & again.
"Maybe he's not a real person."
Maybe it's not a real purpose.
Maybe my slips are too much
like pratfalls (fat falls).
Maybe the lever is detached from the
mainspring. The billiard ball
burned against the slide
of the toaster (holster). That's no
puzzle it's my knife (slice, life,
pipe). *The Rip that Ricochets around
the Rumor*. As in two's two too
many. "I thought you said haphazard—

but if you did you're wrong."
If you've got your concentration you've got
just about everything worth writing home
that tomorrow came sooner than expected
or put those keys away
unless you intend to use me and
then toss me aside like so much worn
out root beer, root for someone,
Bill, take a chance, give till it
stops hurtling through the fog or
fog substitute.

Save me
So that I can exist

Lose me
So that I may find you

"That's an extremely unripe plum."
"There's no plum like the plum
of concatenation." *Plunge & drift,*
drift & plunge. The streets are
icy with incipience.

Mao Tse Tung Wore Khakis

Who would have thought Paul McCartney would be
the Perry Como of the 1990s?
**The Thunderbirds gleam end-to-end-to-end
in the studio backlot.** The lions
have left their lair and are roaming just by
the subconscious. PP-warning: Illegal
received field on preceding line.
***Bethel/'94: I just don't want any
hippies come in here and steal
my computer.*** *In my experience*
I often misspell words. **Evidently
Bob Dylan missed the exit and ended
up in Saugerties.** You can sell some of
the people most of the time, but you can't

Michael Gottlieb

Timing Is Everything

After I get past the used up part. No thanks, I'll eat them in the car. Probably, I think, they are going to shit on the piano. Custodian in a drum. The one with feather all over his face. In the ashtray. A frog in a Cuisinart. What would we do for eggs then?

Tell me, what do you think of my latest book? One to open a Tab and one to call her father. Moi? You give them a toaster and they give you ten thousand dollars. For that much I get to make my own hole. Pardon me Roy, is that the cat that chewed your new shoes?

The person she was sitting with was Jill Clayburgh. Look at that S car go. We were at the zoo all morning so I thought I'd take them to a movie. A stuffed dermatologist. She calls her father. She makes a reservation. One to make a spritzer and one to call a super. Dead, I thought she was Jewish.

Three hours of begging. The one wearing a clean bowling shirt. With prices like that you won't get very more either. Not since Superman. Because there's no John. So they know when to stop fucking. Cold and clammy and wants to hold your hand. Young and Single and Loose. Jacques Custodian.

It says here you can swim and play tennis and go horseback riding. You can eat a bowling ball. Smelly fate. She's decided to have the county bury her. A branch manager. Atlanta. And don't mess with the rebbetsen again. Yogurt has an active culture. Snap-On Tools. She might put her finger in a dike.

Forget the roses, read the card. But how do you breathe through it? I hate the smell of burning rubber and the sound of screaming women. One Watt. So the Irish wouldn't take over the world. I already gave you a hundred dollars not to talk about that.

Yellow and sits in the corner. It's one prick against a thousand. No, but the last guy was sick. You call him Sir. It just goes to show that if you give the people what they want they'll come out for it. If you know the punch line then it's funny. Licking everyone on the court.

Vinegar and water on the rocks, please. Don't worry about fly in your soup, sir, there's a spider on your bread; he'll take care of it. The first telephone Pole. It has more hops because it's from Australia. Because that's the one day a year that Jerry Lewis works.

Anything but the electric eels. If she was manager of a Burger King then she'd always have it her way. Fixed or repaired daily. It's alright now but what about when the tide comes in? Have you ever thought of being a plumber? I just pushed him down the first step, he fell all the rest. By the wrist and ankles.

Julie Patton

      word
A. first poem (is a letter)

    B. shat
      spiss(t) scat
    buss off
    (maw, maw)

  B to Meter
  a   blood of the lamb
  l
  d
  w
  in

       where only begroes
       to name

This tune
          teenth
talented
         Bribel
  belt.

A … aft ri can can
     on the lamb

    is lamb

                    Bee Vomit

Kevin Davies

  —] Keep losing things
discovered on Mars.
Forced to back down
from what wasn't your position in the first place
Or mine either [

] "... never to return."

  — "Let me think." [   ]agnificent

ashtray. Me my
money. My money in a bag
of. Here the

voice of the marred! [*No más, no*

más.] "I don't want the cat to love me."

— **plot.** but the people she gives it to

plot. [b]ut prayer focused [
         ] kept ambition sharp. **plot**

everybody dies

The citizen-evangelists go boating
In [   ] synthetic opals
[A]nd all you can steal.

Can't think of the word I [

                                        ] Tracheotomy.

— **plot.** We are studying the folk tale. Whatever you think,
this life is dedicated to out-&-out beer. Burger
specials are predicated on people being unable to resist [**plot**] to
cut the grease. Thus
there is a disorder within the classification of
Culture & Nature. Your baby doesn't love you
any more. Every night I am in Vietnam.

         The psycho-thriller bursts from the outside-in

                    of a previous decade
                         Let it end

              & another begin in its vulnerable middle.

— some middle-distance cairn that, when approached, becomes just another dumb hill town looking to increase its market share.

[   ] worse, the inner world or the outer world?

Dolphin endorphins.

can't've been transcribed, I

— *career move*. fake insanity. Nevertheless you will die & it won't work. In any group of three or more, one is the dad. & reappear, transformed, in later archive. *get me the remote-control device, dammit.* All the little attachments on this[   ] have names. *updated synopsis.* the white elephants selling us the market. All the trailer hitches [J. Edgar Hoover, in conversation] have meanings.

— hometowns are [*psychological*]

— hometowns are [*mistaken in their assumptions*]

— hometowns are [*retirements meccas*]

From each according to the vituperative whiplash of each understanding, to each according to the brazenness of each exotic fourth toe, elongated & erectile in a state-withered world of contemplative dalliance. VIVA CLASS HATE! Rules? We'll look back some day from the apex of the jetpack trajectory & recognize the mannerism for what's opaque of its method, be measured by its upward regard of our proclivities, as lost to each other as toast to breakfast on the '86 death shuttle. Coin on a string in human holes. Dèbris plucked from landfill placed perhaps as offering on futon—END TRANSMISSION OVER—

The thrill of being misquoted, of inserting miniature cars in the urethra

I'm sorry, but I don't speak Russian.

        They look like

Emergency fire exits but actually

           They're weapons.

Stacy Doris

from Artic Uncles (on Rollerblades)
Advance

Probe droids SUCK!

Unc. helped Yann with the igloo setup,

popsicle version.

Soothing: "Don't worry: the sounds are way distant."

As ice thins—

the background shakes—

obfuscating *Leap of Wrath*.

Live die and what not.
Lie down and crawl off.

Available (echo) AVAILABLY:

Tundra Blitz:

OH SWEET,

AGENT madness, bit of Latin revenge (yes-'um asked for)

New World Comp #.

Mighty Virgin Alert.

MUNCHED ON THE LAGOON . . .

(blued) elkboys autosuck

flammable?

Why the hat?

TiK glides, from snowcap, down to their mobile

(with a (cold) pizza)

Chanted:

GORE OX Chris Scissor
  8   8   6   8

In playability and shift.

Enthused, Uncle orders

un psycho-style salon

for to reverse the brains of two *lassies*

sipping insults

'til they're sugar-crazed, hot

and see what's on their minds:

neck-tethered, caressed to pieces.

Laments: *MY icon bean—Neurospunk—*

(Half-man but all caution):

hamburgering over it

(a nanosplit dawning)

TAKES RIDES

(sonic female champ)

IV VR TM

...Mmmmmm, ask the Virtutects.

Overhead arrival: Hey!

Adrenaline-hot mam's'

twit vision

priestly, glazed as all that.

SO, Urethraejacked boy-bomb:

Any further questions?

In double-come electrodes, Unc.

was choo-choo-spliced out. Yep.

Later Able-mapped suburb, with colorless bilge ancient . . .

QUICK *the jar:*

messages: Wait for *Me* specter

while Matrix is Navigate

 (the ethanol champs)

A Flash: Smutwalls and pincushions TEAM UP
in a wake, of remedy-scattershot:

Pyramid wolf hide-away.

    Mind-sweeper

      Awesome posse:

    Ask a harem:

                      (echo).

(Lands)

"In next to nothing"

rolled use - whatever—

pointing, 17, tidy-but-hard,

Experienced Richness.

. . . . .

Dizzy 17 prong, solo-attached,

whose needed/ an account of TiK:

Odd, browner, naturally,

glum. Jubilant: where

a bellboy in sight, or belief

at a nature precinct eat quickly!

(Lands)

A serious talk, but with no leg to stand on

bender dummies up/ crush dummies

come along and go to pieces.

In a rush careen bounty scam

upsets the creature model.

A HOMUNCULUS VIEWPOINT

(realistic fluid) moves

 (in this case, small)

inch by inch!

Face out.

X-tra Innings: The Twins' Last Metamorphosis

Three doggie tornadoes

crop up record firing

along—too bad for them—soporific hillsides.

Leap from the skateboard

jiggle positions

(they're heavy).

Elsewhere Poodle Gorgeous

bobs in unknown platforms

helplessly jell-o.

Ingenious Pleasures

Contributors

Kathy Acker (1947–1997)
Kathy Acker was a novelist, playwright, and essayist who grew up on New York City's Upper East Side. She studied classics at Brandeis University and the University of California, San Diego. Her first work appeared as part of the New York City literary underground of the mid-1970s. Acker often moved back and forth between San Diego, San Francisco, New York, and London. Her writing style and subject matter reflected the New York punk movement of the 1970s and early 1980s. Her novels are textual collages involving the extended use of appropriation and cut-up techniques. They mix pornography, diatribe, parody, politics, and gossip, exploring themes of violence, alienation, and objectified sexuality in a kind of post-punk American nouveau roman. In 1989 she moved to San Francisco and worked as an adjunct professor at the San Francisco Art Institute for several years. She was diagnosed with cancer in 1996. Her books include *The Childlike Life of the Black Tarantula* (1973), *Great Expectations* (1982), *Blood and Guts in High School* (1984), *Don Quixote* (1986), *Empire of the Senseless* (1988), *In Memoriam to Identity* (1990), *Hannibal Lecter, My Father* (1991), *Portrait of an Eye: Three Novels* (1992), *My Mother: Demonology* (1994), *Pussy, King of the Pirates* (1996), and *Essential Acker: The Selected Writings of Kathy Acker* (2002).

Bruce Andrews (b. 1948)
Born in Chicago, Illinois, Bruce Andrews earned a BA and an MA from the Johns Hopkins University and a PhD from Harvard. He moved to New York City in 1975, where he coedited *L=A=N=G=U=A=G=E* magazine with Charles Bernstein. From 1975 to 2013 Andrews taught political science at Fordham University. He has been involved in a long series of collaborative multimedia projects and performances. As composer, sound designer, and live mixer, he has been the music director for Sally Silvers & Dancers since the mid-1980s. Andrews's poetry utilizes a technique involving cards on which he records small groups of phrases and single words, stores them in boxes for months

or years, then sifts and arranges the cards to create new poetry, often with provocative, socially charged results. He is associated with Language poetry. His books include *Edge* (1973), *Film Noir* (1978), *Sonnets* (1980), *Wobbling* (1981), *R + B* (1981), *Love Songs* (1982), *Give 'em Enough Rope* (1987), *Getting Ready to Have Been Frightened* (1988), *I Don't Have any Paper so Shut up; or, Social Romanticism* (1992), *Tizzy Boost* (1993), *Divestiture-A* (1994), *EX WHY ZEE* (1995), *Lip Service* (2001), *Swoon Noir* (2007), and *You Can't Have Everything . . . Where Would You Put It!* (2011). His essays are collected in *Paradise & Method: Poetics & Praxis* (1996).

Guillaume Apollinaire (1880–1918)
French poet, playwright, short-story writer, novelist, and art critic Guillaume Apollinaire (pseudonym of Guillelmus Apollinaris de Kostrowitzki) was born in Rome, the son of a Polish émigrée and possibly an Italian officer. He was raised in the French Riviera and educated in Monaco and Nice. By the age of eighteen, Apollinaire had settled in Paris. His first collection of poetry was *L'enchanteur pourrissant* (1909), but it was *Alcools* (1913) that established his reputation for stylistic experimentation and novelty of subjects and themes. In 1914 Apollinaire enlisted during World War I, becoming a second lieutenant in the French infantry. He suffered a head wound in 1916 and was discharged back to Paris, where he saw the staging of his drama *Les mamelles de Tiresias: Drame surrealiste* (The Breasts of Tiresias) and published a novella, *The Poet Assassinated*, and a collection of typographically arranged images-poems, *Calligrammes* (1918). Apollinaire died of Spanish influenza in 1918. In 1947, Francis Poulenc produced Apollinaire's *Les mamelles de Tiresias: Drame surrealiste*—the first work to call itself Surrealist—as an opera.

John Ashbery (1927–2017)
John Ashbery was a poet, critic, and translator born in Rochester, New York. After graduating from Harvard in 1949 and receiving an MA from Columbia, Ashbery lived in Paris until 1965, writing art criticism for the *New York Herald-Tribune* and *Art News*. Returning to New York, he was the executive editor of *Art News* from 1965 to 1972 and taught at Brooklyn College. In later years he divided his time between New York City and Hudson, New York. Ashbery's poetry is characterized by free-flowing linguistic play and collagelike shifts in tone and subject, often with an undercurrent of deadpan humor. His open-ended, multiphonic style mixes pop culture and high-art allusion in equal

measure, generating a surprising but graceful sense of obliquity. Ashbery was part of the New York School of poetry. His many books include *Some Trees* (1956), *The Tennis Court Oath* (1962), *Rivers and Mountains* (1966), *The Double Dream of Spring* (1970), *Three Poems* (1972), *Self-Portrait in a Convex Mirror* (1975), *Houseboat Days* (1977), *A Wave* (1984), *Flow Chart* (1991), *Can You Hear, Bird* (1995), *Girls on the Run* (1999), *Chinese Whispers* (2002), *Breezeway* (2015), and *Collected Poems, 1956–1987* (2008).

Russell Atkins (b. 1926)

The poet, playwright, editor, and composer Russell Atkins was born in Cleveland, Ohio, and has resided there for most of his life. Raised by his grandmother, mother, and aunt, he developed a love of music and started writing poetry at an early age. Atkins studied music at the Cleveland School of Arts and the Cleveland Institute of Music. In 1950 he cofounded the journal *Free Lance: a magazine of poetry and prose*, which ran until 1980, gaining a worldwide readership. Atkins's work often crosses over traditional divisions of form, genre, and style. Music is central to his writing methods. "I would compose like a painter and write poems like a composer," he once said. Atkins developed a mode of composition he calls "phenomenalism," in which image and sound combinations extend the possibilities of meaning through sonic play and visual forms. He has also often been associated with the concrete poetry movement. Atkins's books include *Phenomena* (1961), *Objects* (1963), *The Abortionist & The Corpse* (verse plays, 1963), *Heretofore* (1968), *Maleficum* (1971), *Objects 2* (1973), *Here in The* (1976), *Russell Atkins: On the Life and Work of an American Master* (2013), and *World'd Too Much: The Poetry of Russell Atkins* (2019).

Charles Bernstein (b. 1950)

Charles Bernstein is a poet, essayist, editor, and scholar. He was born in New York City and educated at the Bronx High School of Science and at Harvard. Together with Bruce Andrews, he edited *L=A=N=G=U=A=G=E* magazine from 1978 to 1981. From 1989 to 2003 he taught at the State University of New York at Buffalo, where he was cofounder and director of the Poetics Program. There he cofounded the Electronic Poetry Center. From 2003 to 2019 Bernstein taught at the University of Pennsylvania, where he cofounded the poetry audio archive PennSound. His poetry uses a heterogeneous mixture of voices and speech registers that includes politics, pop culture, advertising, literary jargon, corporate-speak, and parody, and it is by turns serious and irreverent.

Bernstein has published several collections of essays: *Content's Dream: Essays 1975–1984* (1986), *A Poetics* (1992), *My Way: Speeches and Poems* (1999), *Pitch of Poetry* (2016), and *Attack of the Difficult Poems* (2011). He is associated with Language poetry. His poetry books include *Asylums* (1975), *Parsing* (1976), *Shade* (1978), *Poetic Justice* (1979), *Senses Of Responsibility* (1979), *Controlling Interests* (1980), *Islets/Irritations* (1983), *The Sophist* (1987), *Rough Trades* (1991), *Dark City* (1994), *Republics of Reality: 1975–1995* (2000), *With Strings* (2001), *Shadowtime* (libretto 2005), *Girly Man* (2006), *All the Whiskey in Heaven* (2010), *Recalculating* (2013), *Near/Miss* (2018), and *Topsy-Turvy* (2021).

Ted Berrigan (1934–1983)
Ted Berrigan was born in Providence, Rhode Island, and attended Providence College for a year before joining the US Army and serving in the Korean War. He received a BA and an MA from the University of Tulsa and moved to New York City in the early 1960s. He published *C Magazine* and "C" Press Books, wrote art criticism, and collaborated with other writers and artists. Aside from years teaching at universities outside New York, Berrigan spent the rest of his life in New York City. He published *The Sonnets* in 1964, which mixed pop culture with high-art references, creating a collage of cadences and voices infused with his sense of humor and gracefulness. Berrigan traced his lineage to the Beat movement and the American Expressionist tradition. He married the poet Alice Notley, and they had two sons, Anselm and Edmund. He is associated with the New York School of poetry. His books include *The Sonnets* (1964), *Bean Spasms* (with Ron Padgett and Joe Brainard, 1967), *Red Wagon* (1976), *Train Ride* (1978), *So Going Around Cities: New &, Selected Poems 1958–1979* (1980), *A Certain Slant of Sunlight* (1988), *The Collected Poems of Ted Berrigan* (2007), and *Get the Money! Collected Prose (1961–1983)* (2022).

Jim Brodey (1942–1993)
Poet and rock-music critic Jim Brodey was born in Brooklyn, New York. He wrote articles for *Crawdaddy!* and other music magazines and interviewed Jimi Hendrix for *San Diego Free Press* and Captain Beefheart for *Rolling Stone*. He edited *Clothesline* magazine and published Jim Brodey Books. He traveled through the Southwest and along the West Coast until settling in Hollywood for an attempt at scriptwriting. In 1976 he moved back to New York City. His work mixes pop culture with erudite music references in a kind of Rimbaudian psychedelia. He was known for his performative reading style. In the

late 1980s he struggled with addiction and was also diagnosed with AIDS. He moved to the San Francisco Bay Area in 1991, where he got sober and served as a volunteer counselor for hospitalized AIDS patients. Brodey died at age fifty from complications related to AIDS. A robust selection of his work appeared in the posthumous *Heart of the Breath*, comprised of poems from 1979 until his death. He also wrote an unpublished novel, *The Horrible*. Brodey was associated with the New York School of poetry. His poetry books include *Identikit* (1967), *Blues of the Egyptian Kings* (1975), *Piranha Yoga* (1977), and *Judyism* (1980).

Clark Coolidge (b. 1939)

Clark Coolidge is a poet and jazz drummer born and raised in Providence, Rhode Island. He has lived, among other places, in Manhattan; San Francisco; Rome; Providence, Rhode Island; Cambridge, Massachusetts; and the Berkshire Hills. He currently lives in Petaluma, California. He coedited *Joglars* magazine from 1964 to 1966 with Michael Palmer. In San Francisco, he played drums in David Meltzer's band, the Serpent Power. From 1969 to 1970 Coolidge produced a weekly poetry show, *Words*, for KPFA in Berkeley, and made word-tapes at Mills College Tape Center. His poetry employs multiple approaches, including cut-up techniques, minimalism, and a kind of extended, improvisational verbal music. Coolidge has been connected to the New York School and the Language poetry movements. Among his dozens of volumes are *Flag Flutter and U.S. Electric* (1966), *Ing* (1969), *Space* (1970), *The Maintains* (1974), *Polaroid* (1975), *Quartz Hearts* (1978), *Own Face* (1978), *Mine: The One That Enters the Stories* (1982), *Solution Passage* (1986), *The Crystal Text* (1986), *At Egypt* (1988), *Sound as Thought* (1990), *Own Face* (1993), *The ROVA Improvisations* (1994), *Now It's Jazz: Writings on Kerouac & the Sounds* (1999), *On the Nameways* (2001), *88 Sonnets* (2012), and *Act of Providence* (2010).

Kevin Davies (b. 1958)

Kevin Davies was born in Nanaimo, British Columbia, Canada. In the 1980s he was active in the Vancouver poetry community and the Kootenay School of Writing collective, a school also associated with Lisa Robertson, Jeff Derksen, and Fred Wah, among others. In the early 1990s he moved to New York City. He currently lives in Brooklyn and works as an editor. Davies's work mixes language from different registers and jargons, combining techniques of postmodern cut-up with classical rhetorical devices, allusion, micronarratives, witticisms, jokes, slogans, détournements, advertising, and melodramatic camp, all delivered with comedic eloquence and formal ingenuity. The results are a giddy but trenchant, frame-shifting sci-fi/punk commentary on neoliberalism. He is the author of *Pause Button* (1992), *Comp.* (2000), *The Golden Age of Paraphernalia* (2008), and *FPO* (2020).

Stacy Doris (1962–2012)
Stacy Doris was a poet and translator born in Bridgeport, Connecticut. She received her BA in literature and society from Brown University and an MFA from the University of Iowa. A translator of French and Spanish, she coedited anthologies of French writing in translation including *Twenty One New (to North America) French Writers* (1997) and *Violence of the White Page* (1991). She lived in New York, Paris, and, for the last ten years of her life, San Francisco, where she taught in the Creative Writing Program at San Francisco State University. She married poet Chet Wiener in 1992. Her work involves a unique inventiveness, wit, and playfulness, using appropriations based on classical forms, pastiche, and parody, often with a wacky and audacious charm. In her work prose, verse, dialogue, and song combine together, bound by an eclectic poetic pleasure principle. Her books include *Kildare* (1995), *Comment Aimer* (1998), *La Vie de Chester Steven Wiener écrite par sa femme* (1998), *Paramour* (2000), *Une Année à New York avec Chester* (2000), *Conference* (2001), *Cheerleader's Guide to the World: Council Book* (2006), *Parlement: Une cométragédie* (2005), *Knot* (2006), *Paramour trans. Anne Portugal and Caroline Dubois* (2009), *The Cake Part* (2011), and *Fledge: a Phenomenology of Spirit* (2012).

Edward Dorn (1929–1999)
Edward Dorn was a poet and novelist born in Illinois, educated at the University of Illinois and Black Mountain College. Dorn's childhood during the Great Depression was marked by the transient migrant life of his mother and stepfather. After graduation Dorn's family settled in Washington state, the setting for his autobiographical novel *By the Sound* (1971). In 1965 Dorn moved to England and taught at the University of Essex. Beginning in 1977, Dorn taught at the University of Colorado at Boulder, where he lived for the rest of his life. His magnum opus, *Gunslinger* (1968), is an unclassifiable epic poem involving a cowboy poet anti-hero roaming across an indefinite modern landscape. Its narrators include the madam of a saloon and a talking horse named Claude Levi-Strauss. Dorn's work is metaphysical and crude, high and low. It mixes the slangy and the grandiloquent, esoteric knowledge and pop

culture. Dorn is associated with the Black Mountain poets. Among his many books are *The Newly Fallen* (1961), *From Gloucester Out* (1964), *Geography* (1965), *The North Atlantic Turbine* (1967), *Recollections of Gran Apacheria* (1974), *Collected Poems: 1956–1974* (1975), *Hello, La Jolla* (1978), *Abhorrences* (1989), *Way West: Stories, Essays and Verse Accounts, 1963–1993* (1993), *Chemo Sábe* (2001), *Collected Poems*, and *Carcanet Press* (2012).

Kenward Elmslie (1929–2022)

Kenward Elmslie was a poet, librettist, and lyricist born in New York City to the daughter of newspaper magnate Joseph Pulitzer. He spent his childhood in Washington, DC, and Colorado. After graduating from Harvard in 1950, he started writing librettos for the Jack Beeson operas *The Sweet Bye and Bye* (1957) and *Lizzie Borden* (1965). In 1952 Elmslie started a relationship with Broadway librettist John Latouche. They bought a farmhouse in Calais, Vermont, and the two divided their time between New York City and Calais until Latouche's death in 1956. Elmslie continued to write lyrics for musicals, including *The Grass Harp* (1971) and *Postcards on Parade* (1999). In 1963 he began a relationship with Joe Brainard, an artist and writer with whom he collaborated on many projects. Elmslie's wild, hilarious, collagelike writing, often combined with the work of painters and other visual artists, mostly defies categorization. In the 1970s he founded Z Press, which published a journal and books. He is associated with the New York School of poetry. His books include *Pavilions* (1961), *Album* (1969), *Motor Disturbance*, (1971), *Girl Machine* (1971), *The Orchid Stories* (a novel, 1973), *Tropicalism* (1975), *Moving Right Along* (1980), *Bare Bones* (1995), and *Routine Disruptions* (1998). His many collaborations with artists include *The Champ* (with Joe Brainard, 1968) and *Cyberspace* (with Trevor Winkfield, 2000).

Baroness Elsa von Freytag-Loringhoven (1874–1927)

Born Elsa Hildegard Plötz in Germany, Elsa von Freytag-Loringhoven moved to the USA in the early 1910s, eventually living in New York City's Greenwich Village in the years before and after the first World War. The first American Dadaist, von Freytag-Loringhoven was called the mother of Dada. She was an innovator in poetic form, sculpture, performance, and fashion, creating elaborate costumes from found objects and fusing collage, fashion, and performance. She wore a bra made out of tomato cans, a necklace made from a bird cage with a canary inside, teaspoon earrings, and postage stamps as makeup. She strode through the streets of New York with her arms covered with rings stolen from local stores, wearing a feathered helmet and a striped leotard—she was punk rock long before punk rock. The Baroness was a crucial innovator in assemblage and found objects, renewing art using otherwise overlooked materials. Though her poems first appeared in *The Little Review* in 1918, most of her poetic output remained unpublished until the appearance of *Body Sweats: The Uncensored Writings of Elsa von Freytag-Loringhoven* in 2011.

Abraham Lincoln Gillespie (1895–1950)
Abraham Lincoln Gillespie, known to his friends as "Link," was born in South Philadelphia's Twenty-Sixth Ward. He attended Penn State University and then transferred to the University of Pennsylvania, where he graduated in 1918 with a degree in College Courses for Teachers. In 1920, not long after he had begun his teaching career, Gillespie had a serious automobile accident that impaired his vision and permanently injured his left leg. The accident, according to many who knew him, also altered his personality. In 1922 Gillespie moved to Paris, where he became friends with composer George Antheil and moved in the expatriate circles of Gertrude Stein and James Joyce. He was part of the group of writers associated with the Paris-based literary magazine *Transition*. His writing involved highly personal and inventive verbal experimentations, eschewing standard spelling and punctuation and incorporating symbols and drawings resembling musical notation. Gillespie's essay "Music Starts a Geometry" appeared in 1927, and he continued to contribute to *Transition* until 1932. Gillespie moved back to Philadelphia's Washington Square neighborhood in 1934. The only book published during his lifetime was *The Shaper* (1948). His collection *The Syntactic Revolution* was published in 1980.

Michael Gottlieb (b. 1951)
Michael Gottlieb is a poet, essayist, and memoirist who was born in the Bronx and grew up in Westchester County, New York. He graduated from Bennington College, where he studied poetry and painting. He has worked for a private detective agency and in business affairs for Warner Bros. Gottlieb divides his time between New York City and Connecticut. He was the publisher of Case/Casement Books (1981–1999) and an editor for *Roof* magazine. Gottlieb's principal themes include language, the city, and the life of poets. His work ranges from early collaged and chance operation poetry to later staged dramatic pieces. His *Memoir and Essay* (2010) is a personal history of his

coming of age as a poet, the evolution of Language poetry, and New York City in the 1970s. Other prose works include *Letters to A Middle Aged Poet* (2012) and *What We Do: Essays for Poets* (2016). He is associated with Language poetry. His poetry books include *Local Color/Eidetic Deniers* (1978), *Pantographic* (1980), *Ninety-Six Tears* (1981), *New York* (1993), *Valu Pac*, (1996), *The Night Book* (1998), *Gorgeous Plunge*, (1999), *Careering Obloquy* (2002), *Lost and Found* (2003), *The Likes Of US* (2007), *The Dust* (2011), *Dear All* (2013), *I Had Every Intention* (2014), *Mostly Clearing* (2019), and *Selected Poems* (2021).

Richard Huelsenbeck (1892–1974)

Richard Huelsenbeck was a poet, journalist, novelist, and psychoanalyst born in Germany. He studied literature and art history in Munich and met Hugo Ball there. After leaving Munich for Berlin in 1914, where he studied medicine, Huelsenbeck moved to Zurich in 1915 and joined the Cabaret Voltaire, where he coined the term "dada." Huelsenbeck returned to Berlin in 1917 and was closely involved with Berlin Dada, doing extravagant performances where he accompanied his poetry with a large drum. He wrote the novel *China Devours People* (1930). With Hitler's rise to power in 1933, Huelsenbeck was expelled from the German writer's union and forbidden to write. He took a job as a ship's surgeon to escape Germany, eventually settling in New York, where he changed his name to Charles R. Hulbeck and was granted a New York State medical license with the help of Albert Einstein. He decided to practice psychiatry, underwent analysis with Karen Horney, and later lectured at the Karen Horney Institute. Huelsenbeck was the editor of *Dada Almanach* and wrote *Dada siegt, En Avant Dada* and other Dadaist works. In 1969 he retired from his psychiatric practice and returned to Switzerland. His autobiography about Zurich and Berlin Dada, *Memoirs of a Dada Drummer*, was published in 1974.

Kenneth Koch (1925–2002)

Kenneth Koch was born in Cincinnati, Ohio, and began writing poems at an early age. A poet, playwright, and fiction writer, Koch also published several books about teaching poetry. He served in the South Pacific during World War II and attended Columbia University, where he studied with Delmore Schwartz. In 1950 Koch went to Paris and Aix-en-Provence as a Fulbright fellow. In 1959 he joined the English and Comparative Literature department at Columbia, and he was a member of the faculty there for many years. His poetry often employs satire, irony, playfulness in both tone and technique, and comic elements suffused with ebullient absurdity. Koch, especially in his earlier work, would often make poetry out of unlikely, poetry-resistant materials. Koch was associated with the New York School of poetry. His many books include *Ko, or A Season on Earth* (1959), *Thank You And Other Poems* (1962), *When the Sun Tries to Go On* (1969), *The Pleasures of Peace: And Other Poems* (1969), *The Art of Love* (1975), *The Duplications* (1977), *New Addresses* (2000), *Straits* (1998), and *The Collected Poems of Kenneth Koch* (2007).

Jackson Mac Low (1922–2004)
Jackson Mac Low was a poet, a composer, and a writer of performance pieces, essays, plays, and radio works. He was born in Chicago and attended the University of Chicago. After graduating, he moved to New York City, where he lived for the rest of his life. His poetry explored "chance operations"—processes involving the generation of random arrangements of words that incorporate language drawn from previously published texts. In 1963 he copublished (with La Monte Young) *An Anthology of Chance Operations*, which became a resource for the Fluxus art movement, of which Mac Low was a founding member. He has collaborated with many composers, musicians, and poets, including Anne Tardos, a visual and performance artist he married in 1990. He published over thirty books and released an album, *Open Secrets* (1993). His books include *The Pronouns—A Collection of 40 Dances—For the Dancers* (1964), *Stanzas for Iris Lezak* (1972), *Asymmetries 1-260* (1980), *Representative Works: 1938–1985* (1986), *Twenties: 100 Poems* (1991), *Pieces o' Six: Thirty-three Poems in Prose* (1992), *Barnesbook* (1996), *154 Forties* (2012), *The Complete Light Poems* (2015), and *Thing of Beauty: New and Selected Works* (2009).

Mina Loy (1882–1966)
Mina Loy was born in London and studied art in England and Germany. She was a poet, playwright, novelist, and artist who moved among the metropolitan centers of modernism in Paris, London, Florence, Berlin, and New York. She is associated with multiple twentieth-century avant-garde movements, including Futurism and Dadaism. In 1915 she published "Love Songs" in the journal *Others*. In 1916 she moved to New York and joined the New York City avant-garde movement there. Her poems were published in the magazines *Little Review*, *Others*, and *The Dial*. In 1923, Loy returned to Paris, where she published *Lunar Baedecker* (1923) and ran a design business and retail shop,

where she marketed her original lampshade designs. She moved back to New York in 1936, leaving the city in 1953 to live with her daughters in Aspen, Colorado. In her lifetime, Loy published two books, *Lunar Baedecker* in 1923 and *Lunar Baedeker and Time Tables* in 1958, as well as many poems, plays, and essays in little magazines. Posthumous collections include *The Last Lunar Baedeker* (1982), *The Lost Lunar Baedeker: Poems of Mina Loy* (1996), the novel *Insel* (1991), and *Stories and Essays of Mina Loy* (2011).

Bernadette Mayer (b. 1945–2022)
Bernadette Mayer was born in Brooklyn, New York, and spent most of her life in New York City. Mayer edited the journal *0 TO 9* with Vito Acconci. From 1978 to 1984 she coedited United Artists books and magazine with her then-partner Lewis Warsh. She served as the director of the St. Mark's Poetry Project from 1980 to 1984. Mayer is known for creating hybrid literary forms that combine poetry, stream-of-consciousness prose, textual-visual art, and journal writing. In 1971 she created the exhibit *Memory*, a collection of photographs displayed with a multipart narration that was created as she remembered the context of each image. The text of *Memory* was a transcription of this narration. *Memory* paved the way for later book-length projects, such as *Midwinter Day* (1982), composed on a single day spent in Lenox, Massachusetts. Mayer is associated with the New York School of poetry and conceptual art. Her books include *Story* (1968), *Moving* (1971), *Memory* (1975), *Studying Hunger* (1976), *Poetry* (1976), *Erudition ex Memoria* (1977), *The Golden Book of Words* (1978), *Utopia* (1984), *Sonnets* (1989), *A Bernadette Mayer Reader* (1992), *The Desire of Mothers to Please Others in Letters* (1994), *Another Smashed Pinecone* (1998), *Two Haloed Mourners* (1998), *Works and Days* (2016), and *Eating The Colors Of A Lineup Of Words* (2015).

Steve McCaffery (b. 1947)
Steve McCaffery is a poet, critic, and performer born in Sheffield, England. He spent his youth in the United Kingdom, earning a BA in English and philosophy from Hull University, an MA from York University in Toronto, and a PhD from SUNY Buffalo in New York. He moved to Toronto in 1968, and in 1970 he began to collaborate with Rafael Barreto-Rivera, Paul Dutton, and bpNichol, forming the sound poetry group the Four Horsemen. McCaffery has also been active in the Toronto Research Group. He has worked extensively in concrete and sound poetry, and his visual poetry has been widely

anthologized. McCaffery has lived in Buffalo since 2004, where he is a professor at SUNY Buffalo and the director of the Poetics Program. His poetry books include *Dr. Sadhu's Muffins* (1974), *Ow's Waif* (1975), *Intimate Distortions* (1979), *Knowledge Never Knew* (1983), *Panopticon* (1984), *Evoba* (1987), *The Black Debt* (1989), *Theory of Sediment* (1991), *Modern Reading: Poems 1969–1990* (1992), *The Cheat of Words* (1996), *Seven Pages Missing: Selected Texts Volume One and Two* (2001, 2002), *The Basho Variations* (2007), *Slightly Left of Thinking* (2008), *Alice In Plunderland* (2015), *Parsival* (2015), and *Dark Ladies* (2016). Together with bpNichol, he edited *Sound Poetry: A Catalogue for the Eleventh International Sound Poetry Festival* (1978).

Taylor Mead (1924–2013)
Born in Grosse Pointe, Michigan, the poet and actor Taylor Mead was part of the Beat poetry scene in San Francisco. After director Ron Rice witnessed Mead jumping onto a bar and yelling out his poetry to the crowd, the two began a collaboration that resulted in the 1960 film *The Flower Thief*. In 1963 Mead moved to New York City and began working with Andy Warhol. That same year, Mead won an Obie Award for his performance in Frank O'Hara's play *The General Returns from One Place to Another*. Warhol featured Mead in many films, including *Tarzan and Jane Regained . . . Sort Of* (1963), *The Nude Restaurant* (1967), *Imitation of Christ* (1967), and *Lonesome Cowboys* (1969). Mead produced several volumes of writing between 1961 and 2005, work that melded together irreverent, sometimes hilarious poetry, diary entries, and aphorisms. His books include *Taylor Mead on Amphetamine and in Europe: Excerpts from the Anonymous Diary of a New York Youth* (1968), *Son of Andy Warhol* (1986), and *A Simple Country Girl* (2005). In his later years Mead lived on Ludlow Street in New York City and read his poetry at a weekly performance at the Bowery Poetry Club.

Frank O'Hara (1926–1966)
Frank O'Hara was a poet, playwright, and art critic who grew up in Massachusetts, studied piano at the New England Conservatory in Boston, and served in the South Pacific during World War II. He attended Harvard and the University of Michigan. In 1951 O'Hara moved to New York City and started working at the Museum of Modern Art, becoming first an assistant and then an associate curator in 1965. O'Hara was deeply involved in the New York art scene and befriended Abstract Expressionist painters who became

a major source of inspiration. His long poem "Second Avenue" shows many techniques he drew from Abstract Expressionism. O'Hara's poetry employed broad and personal inclusiveness, bringing in "unpoetic" materials like quotations, gossip, and commercials and often deploying a charming, witty tone. He drew from nonliterary sources, including jazz, and incorporated Surrealistic and Dadaistic techniques alongside colloquial speech and a dynamic, flexible syntax. He was a member of the New York School of poets. O'Hara's books include *Meditations in an Emergency* (1956), *Lunch Poems* (1964), and *The Collected Poems of Frank O'Hara* (1971). Frank O'Hara was killed in an accident while vacationing on Fire Island. He was forty years old.

Peter Orlovsky (1933–2010)

Peter Orlovsky was born on the Lower East Side and grew up in Northport, New York. His father was a Russian immigrant. The family was impoverished, and both parents were alcoholics who eventually separated. Orlovsky's younger brother Julius was a schizophrenic who Peter helped support into adulthood. Orlovsky attended high school in Queens but dropped out to help support his family by working as an orderly at a mental hospital. Drafted in 1953 during the Korean War, after Orlovsky told an officer, "An army with guns is an army against love," he was sent to San Francisco to serve as a medic. While working as a painter's model, he met Allen Ginsberg and began a relationship that lasted until Ginsberg's death in 1997. Orlovsky began writing poetry in 1957 while living in Paris. His work features an outsider style and originality that includes alternate spellings of words, bluntness, unliterary materials, and a unique sense of poetic glee. Orlovsky was a member of the Beat movement. His books include *Dear Allen, Ship will land Jan 23, 58* (1971), *Lepers Cry* (1972), *Clean Asshole Poems & Smiling Vegetable Songs* (1978), *Straight Hearts' Delight: Love Poems and Selected Letters* (with Allen Ginsberg, 1980), and *Peter Orlovsky, a Life in Words* (2014).

Rochelle Owens (b. 1936)

Rochelle Owens is a poet and playwright born in Brooklyn, New York. She graduated from Lafayette High School in 1953 and moved to Manhattan, where she briefly studied poetry at the New School and acting at HB Studio. She became a part of the Beat scene in Greenwich Village, as well as part of the early ethnopoetics movement, and eventually became involved with the start of the St. Mark's Poetry Project and Deux Megot reading series.

She married the poet George Economou in 1962. Known as a pioneer of the experimental off-off-Broadway theater movement during the 1960s and 1970s, Owens premiered plays at the Judson Poets Theatre, La MaMa Experimental Theatre Club, and Theater for the New City. Her poetry books include *Not Be Essence That Cannot Be* (1961), *Salt and Core* (1968), *I Am the Babe of Joseph Stalin's Daughter: Poems, 1961–71* (1972), *Poems from Joe's Garage* (1973), *The Joe Eighty-Two Creation Poems* (1974), *French Light* (1984), *How Much Paint Does The Painting Need* (1988), *Black Chalk* (1992), *Solitary Workwoman* (2011), *Out of Ur—New & Selected Poems 1961–2012* (2012), and *Hermaphropoetics, Drifting Geometries* (2017).

Julie Patton (b. 1956)

Julie Ezelle Patton is a poet, permaculturist, performer, and visual artist born in Cleveland, Ohio. She received her BFA from Antioch College in 1979. Her poetics take the form of music, print, handwriting, drawing, design, altered books, scrolls, extended texts, music performance, and site-specific installations. Patton's performance work emphasizes improvisation and collaboration and bridges literary and musical composition. She has performed at many international venues and festivals and is a frequent collaborator with choreographers, poets, filmmakers, and composers. She is the founding director of Let It Bee Green Space & Arc Hives, a D-I-Y eco-arts artist-housing project foregrounding creative utilitarian projects, field-literacy, ritual maintenance work, neighborhood love economies, and food for the soul in Cleveland. Patton has taught at New York University, Naropa University, Cooper Union, Case Western University, and Teachers & Writers Collaborative. She splits her time between New York City and Cleveland. Her books include *Teething on Type* (1996), *A Garden Per Verse (or What Else do You Expect from Dirt?)* (1999), *Notes for Some (Nominally) Awake* (2007), *Using Blue To Get Black* (2008), and *Writing With Crooked Ink* (2015).

Bob Perelman (b. 1947)

Bob Perelman is a poet, critic, and translator born in Youngstown, Ohio. He matriculated at the University of Rochester as a prospective concert pianist but later changed his major from music to classics. In 1969 he moved to Iowa City, where he received an MFA from the University of Iowa, then he returned to Michigan for an MA in Greek and Latin. He also received a PhD from the University of California at Berkeley. Perelman edited *Hills* magazine as well as two anthologies of speeches by poets: *Writing/Talks* (1985) and *Talks* (1980). His approach to poetry combines historical reference, politics, and popular culture, often delivered with humor and irony. He has collaborated extensively with his wife, the painter Francie Shaw. Perelman published the critical studies *The Marginalization of Poetry* (1996) and *The Trouble with Genius: Reading Pound, Joyce, Stein, and Zukofsky* (1994). His translations appear in *Modern Archaist: Selected Poems of Osip Mandelstam* (2008) and *The Selected Poems of Tomaž Šalamun* (1988). Perelman was a professor at the University of Pennsylvania. He is associated with Language poetry. His books of poetry include *Braille* (1975), *7 Works* (1978), *a.k.a.* (1979), *Primer* (1981), *To the Reader* (1984), *The First World* (1986), *Face Value* (1988), *Captive Audience* (1988), *Virtual Reality* (1993), *The Future of Memory* (1998), *Ten to One—Selected Poems* (1999), *Playing Bodies* (with Francie Shaw 2002), *IFLIFE* (2007), and *Jack and Jill in Troy* (2019).

Francis Picabia (1879–1953)

Francis Picabia was a painter, writer, illustrator, designer, and editor involved with the movements of Cubism, Dadaism, and Surrealism. Notable for his playful, anarchic spirit, his gleeful disregard for conventions, his absurdist humor, and his continuous, unpredictable changes of style, Picabia was born in Paris to a Cuban diplomat father and a French mother. After participating in the 1913 Armory Show in New York City and receiving a solo exhibition at Alfred Stieglitz's gallery "291" in the same year, Picabia moved to New York temporarily and met Marcel Duchamp and Man Ray. Afterward, while living in Barcelona, Picabia published his first volume of poetry and the first issues of *391*, a magazine modeled after Stieglitz's *291*. He published his poems entitled *Cinquante-deux miroirs* (52 Mirrors) in 1917. By the end of World War II, Picabia had returned to Paris, where he resumed painting in an abstract style and writing poetry. In 1925 he left Paris to settle in the south of France, and he returned to Paris in 1945. *I Am a Beautiful Monster: Poetry, Prose, and Provocation*, the first comprehensive edition in English of Picabia's writings, was published in 2012.

Bern Porter (1911–2004)

Bern Porter was a poet, artist, physicist, and publisher born in Maine. In 1935 he moved to New York City to work on cathode-ray tubes. In 1940 Porter was drafted for uranium-separation work on the Manhattan Project. When the United States dropped an atomic bomb on Hiroshima, Porter walked away from the project, realizing his research had been used to create weaponry. Disillusioned with his work as a physicist, he turned to art, developing his own creations that incorporated found poetry, sound poetry, mail art, and performance. His collage poems, which he called "Founds," mixed advertisements, junk mail, scientific documents, instruction booklets, and other materials. *Found Poems* was published in 1972. His other books include *The Wastemaker, The Book of Do's, Dieresis, Here Comes Everybody's Don't Book,* and *Sweet End*. He published work by Henry Miller, Kenneth Patchen, and Anais Nin under his imprint Bern Porter Books. Porter was an active participant in an international mail-art network. He worked again as a physicist on NASA's Saturn V manned space project while working on the integration of science and art—his "Sciart Mainfesto." In 1968 he moved back to Maine from Hunstville, Alabama. *Found Poems* was reprinted in 2012.

Sun Ra (1914–1993)
Born Herman Blount in Birmingham, Alabama, Sun Ra was a major American jazz composer, arranger, bandleader, piano and synthesizer player, poet, and pioneer of Afrofuturism. He attended Alabama Agricultural and Mechanical University on scholarship, but he left for Chicago to pursue music in the 1940s. There he developed a visionary philosophy and art that fused ancient Egyptian mythology and science fiction. He claimed citizenship on the planet Saturn. He relocated his group The Arkestra to New York City in 1961, and again to Philadelphia in 1968. Sun Ra's innovative and far-ranging music reflected the history of jazz, encompassing blues, stride, swing, bebop, hard bop, doo wop, modal jazz, free jazz, and fusion. His discography includes over one hundred full-length albums. The Arkestra's performances involved singers, dancers, costumes of glittering robes, and Egyptian-inspired, space-age headdresses. Their performances often entailed extended durations and included chanting processionals through the audience. His film *Space Is the Place* was released in 1974. Starting in the early 1970s, Sun Ra's poetry has been published as the book *The Immeasurable Equation* in several versions over the years. *The Immeasurable Equation: The Collected Poetry and Prose* was published in 2005. Norton Records released a series of Sun Ra spoken word LPs in 2010.

Tom Raworth (1938–2017)
Tom Raworth was born and raised in South London. He earned an MA in literary translation in 1970 at the University of Essex. As founder of Matrix

Press, cofounder of Goliard Press, and editor of *Outburst* magazine, Raworth helped bring American poetry to English readers. In the 1970s he traveled widely, living in the United States and Mexico before returning to Britain and settling in Cambridge in 1977. Raworth's poetry involves a kaleidoscopic rush of juxtapositions—a stream of interlinking images and thoughts. He draws on surrealism, film, and pop art, sometimes leaning toward minimalism and sometimes employing humor. Raworth wrote several book-length poems using pared-down lines such as *ACE* (1974), *Catacoustics* (1991), and *Writing* (1982). When giving poetry readings he read at a breakneck tempo. He created collages and collaborated with jazz musicians, painters, and poets. Raworth has been associated with Black Mountain, the New York School, and Language poetry. His many books include *The Relation Ship* (1967), *Moving* (1971), *Pleasant Butter* (1972), *Common Sense* (1976), *Heavy Light* (1985), *Visible Shivers* (1987), *Tottering State* (1988), *Eternal Sections* (1993), *Clean & Well Lit* (1996), *Meadow* (1999), *Collected Poems* (2003), *Windmills in Flames* (2010), and *As When: A Selection* (2015).

Aram Saroyan (b. 1943)

Aram Saroyan is a poet, novelist, biographer, memoirist, and playwright born in New York City. He is the son of the author William Saroyan. Aram Saroyan has also lived in Bolinas, California, and Connecticut, among other places. In the 1960s he edited *Lines* magazine and Telegraph Books. He is known for his minimal poems, a form he developed during the 1960s, involving extremely short, sometimes single-word poems which render the reading process instantaneous. George Plimpton included Saroyan's one-word poem "lighght" in *The American Literary Anthology*, which sparked a twenty-year controversy over NEA funding.

Turning to prose in the 1970s, Saroyan focused on biographies and memoirs, including the autobiographical novel *The Street* 1974) and *Genesis Angels: The Saga of Lew Welch and the Beat Generation* (1980). Saroyan is associated with the New York School of poetry and with conceptual art. His poetry books include *Poetry* (1963), *In* (1965), *Top* (1965), *Works* (1966), *Sled Hill Voices* (1966), *Aram Saroyan* (1967), *Coffee Coffee* (1967), *@ 1968* (1968), *Pages* (1969), *Words and Photographs* (1970), *Cloth: An Electric Novel* (1971), *The Rest* (1971), *The Bolinas Books* (1974), *O My Generation, and Other Poems* (1976), *Day and Night: Bolinas Poems* (1998), *Day by Day: Poems and Notes Written in Bolinas in 1973* (2002), and *Complete Minimal Poems* (2007).

Edith Sitwell (1887–1964)

Edith Sitwell was a poet and critic born in Scarborough, Yorkshire, England, the eldest of three literary siblings. Her first book, *The Mother and Other Poems*, appeared in 1915. In 1916 she and her brothers edited the anthology *Wheels*. Her prose works include *Alexander Pope*, *Bath*, *The English Eccentrics*, *A Poet's Notebook*, and *A Notebook on William Shakespeare*. She also wrote a novel based on the life of Jonathan Swift, *I Live Under a Black Sun*. In 1923 her *Facade, An Entertainment*, in which poems were recited through a megaphone from behind a decorated curtain, was set to music by William Walton. Her London Blitz poem "Still Falls the Rain" was set to music by Benjamin Britten. A supporter of innovative trends in English poetry, she turned her flat into a meeting place for young writers, including Dylan Thomas.

Gertrude Stein (1874–1946)

Gertrude Stein was a poet, novelist, playwright, and librettist born in Allegheny, Pennsylvania, of parents of German Jewish descent, and raised in Oakland, California. Stein attended Radcliffe College, studying psychology under William James. After moving to Paris in 1903, she and her brother Leo established a literary and artistic salon at 27 rue de Fleurus, attracting American expatriates whom she dubbed the Lost Generation. Stein met her lifelong companion, Alice B. Toklas, in 1909. By the early 1920s Stein had begun to publish her innovative works: *Three Lives* (1909), *Tender Buttons* (1914), and *The Making of Americans* (1925). Stein employed description to achieve what she called "a continuous present," comparing the technique to a movie camera freezing action into separate frames. Stein extended this technique in *Tender Buttons*, a series of verbal collages closely related to the Cubist painting of Picasso and Juan Gris. Stein also wrote librettos to several operas by Virgil Thompson, notably *Four Saints in Three Acts* and *The Mother of Us All*. Stein's works also include *Stanzas in Meditation*, *The Autobiography of Alice B. Toklas*, and *How to Write*.

Anne Tardos (b. 1943)

Anne Tardos is a poet, composer, and visual and performance artist born in Cannes, France. She grew up in Paris, Budapest, and Vienna, and she moved to New York City in 1966. She met Jackson Mac Low in 1975, and they were later married and began a collaboration composing, writing, and performing poetry and music that lasted until his death. Tardos pioneered a unique multilingual writing style mixing French, Hungarian, German, and English words and passages. Her work also involves multimedia combinations of video stills, photographs, collages, and texts. She has created performance pieces, radio plays, videos, and musical compositions. Her work has been performed or featured at the Museum of Modern Art, the Venice Biennale, and at many international sound-poetry festivals. She lives in Manhattan with her husband, the composer Michael Byron. Her books include *Cat Licked the Garlic* (1992), *Uxudo* (1999), *The Dik-dik's Solitude: New and Selected Works* (2003), *I Am You* (2008), *Both Poems* (2011), *Nine 1-126* (2015), *The Camel's Pedestal* (2017), *The Exploding Nothingness of Never Define* (2020), and *Andante: Scales and Proportions for a Chemical Orchestra Amid the Fraying Norms* (2022).

Tristan Tzara (1896–1963)

Born Samuel Rosenstock, Tristan Tzara was a Romanian-born French poet, essayist, and playwright and one of the founders and central figures of the Dada movement. His first published symbolist poetry appeared in Romanian. Tzara immigrated to Switzerland in 1916, where, with Jean Arp, Hugo Ball, and others, he founded Dadaism and staged performances at the Cabaret Voltaire in Zurich. Tzara left Switzerland in 1919 and settled in Paris, where he collaborated with André Breton and Louis Aragon. His volumes such as *Twenty-Five Poems* (1918) and *Of Our Birds* (1923) fused criticism and poetry to create hybrid literary texts. Tzara's surrealist phase began in the early 1930s. His works published during this period include the epic poem *Approximate Man, and Other Writings* (1931), *The Travelers' Tree* (1930), *Where Wolves Drink* (1932), *The Anti-head* (1933), and *Seed and Bran* (1935). He became an antifascist, a Marxist, and a member of the French Resistance during the Nazi occupation of France. He produced poetry, plays, essays on art and literature, critical commentary, unfinished studies on Villon and Rabelais, and an unfinished autobiographical novel, *Place Your Bets*.

Hannah Weiner (1928–1997)

Hannah Weiner was born in Providence, Rhode Island. She attended Radcliffe College and graduated with a BA in English Literature in 1950. She worked for several publishing houses in New York City and began writing poetry around 1963. She worked as a lingerie designer and as a buyer for dresses at Bloomingdales. In the late 1960s Weiner was part of the visual-arts scene in New York City, a confluence of poets and performance and visual artists including Andy Warhol, Carolee Schneeman, David Antin, and Bernadette Mayer. In the early '70s she began an extended writing practice that she continued for the rest of her life, a series of journals that were "clairvoyantly" dictated, partly the result of her schizophrenia and partly an extension of her technique of mixing discursive strains from different contexts, including hallucinated words. She became one of the writers associated with Language poetry. Her books include *The Magritte Poems* (1970), *Clairvoyant Journal* (1978), *LittleBooks/Indians* (1980), *Nijole's House* (1981), *The Code Poems* (based on international maritime codes, 1982), *Sixteen* (1983), *Spoke* (1984), *Weeks* (1990), *The Fast* (1992), *Silent Teachers Remembered Sequel* (1994), *We Speak Silent* (1996), *Hannah Weiner's* Country Girl—*1971* (2004), and *Open House* (2007).

Williams Carlos Williams (1883–1963)
William Carlos Williams was a poet, novelist, essayist, and playwright associated with modernism and imagism. He was born in Rutherford, New Jersey, of an English father raised in the Dominican Republic. His mother of French extraction was raised in Puerto Rico. Williams began writing poetry while a student at Horace Mann High School in New York City. After receiving his MD from the University of Pennsylvania, he returned to Rutherford, where he had a lifelong medical practice. Some of his poems were written on prescription blanks, others typed in the moments between patient visits. He experimented with poetic forms throughout his career, creating radically innovative poems such as *Kora in Hell* and *Spring and All*, which fused criticism, aphorism, philosophy, and poetry. Williams's works include *Imaginations*, the five-volume epic *Paterson*, and *Pictures from Brueghel and Other Poems*, which was awarded the Pulitzer Prize. He had a significant influence on many of the American literary movements of the 1950s and '60s.

Credits

The following publishers and individuals have graciously granted permission to include the indicated work in this book.

Kathy Acker, from *Essential Acker* (Grove/Atlantic, 2002). © the Estate of Kathy Acker. Used by permission of Grove/Atlantic, Inc. Any third party use of this material, outside of this publication, is prohibited.

Bruce Andrews, "A small bird," from *Edge* (Arry Press, 1973). Reprinted with permission of the author.

Bruce Andrews, selections, from *Divestiture-A* (Drogue Press, 1994). Reprinted with permission of the author.

Bruce Andrews, "Eagles Ate my Estrogen," from *EX WHY ZEE* (Roof Books, 1995). Reprinted with permission of the author.

Apollinaire, "Monday rue Christine," from *Zone* (New York Review of Books, 2015). Translation © 2015 by Ron Padgett.

John Ashbery, "Leaving The Atocha Station," from *The Tennis Court Oath* (Wesleyan University Press, 1977). Reprinted with permission.

Russell Atkins, "Weekend Murder," from *World'd Too Much: The Selected Poetry of Russell Atkins*, edited by Kevin Prufer and Robert E. McDonough (Cleveland State University Poetry Center, 2019). Reprinted with permission of the editors and the Cleveland State University Poetry Center (Caryl Pagel, director).

Charles Bernstein, "Soapy Water" and "Mao Tse Tune Wore Khaki," from *Republics of Reality: 1975–1995* (Sun & Moon Press, 2000). Used with permission of the author.

Charles Bernstein, "Claire-in-the-Building," from *My Way: Speeches and Poems* (University of Chicago Press, 1999). Used with permission of the author.

Ted Berrigan, "Ass Face," from *The Collected Poems of Ted Berrigan*, edited by Alice Notley, with Anselm Berrigan and Edmund Berrigan (University of California Press, 2005). Reprinted with permission of Alice Notley.

Jim Brodey, "Bum Trip," from *Heart of the Breath: Poems 1979–1992*, edited by Clark Coolidge (Hard Press, 1996).

Clark Coolidge, "HEY! YOU LOOK LIKE A GIRL," from *Uncollected and Unpublished Poems, 1966–1968*. Reprinted with permission of the author.

Clark Coolidge, "Acid," from *Flag Flutter & U.S. Electric* (Lines Press, 1966).

Clark Coolidge, "Fed Drapes," "Crisp Loss," and "Machinations Calcite," from *Space* (Harper & Row, 1970). Reprinted with permission of the author.

Clark Coolidge, "Pumper Mouth" and "The Automatic Nerve at Razed Heights," from *On the Nameways*, vol. 1: *The Figures* (2000). Reprinted with permission of the author.

Clark Coolidge, "Gulp," from *On the Nameways*, vol. 2: *The Figures* (2001). Reprinted with permission of the author.

Kevin Davies, "—] Keep losing things," "—**plot.** but the people she gives it to," and "—some middle-distance cairn that, when approached, becomes just another," from *Pause Button* (Tsumani Editions, 1992). Reprinted with permission of the author.

Kevin Davies, "From each according to the vituperative whiplash of each understanding" and "The thrill of being misquoted, of inserting miniature cars in the urethra," from *Thunk* (Situations Press, 1995). Reprinted with permission of the author.

Stacy Doris, from *Kildare* (Roof Books 1994). Reprinted with permission of Chet Wiener.

Ed Dorn, from *Collected Poems* (Carcanet, 2012). Published on behalf of the rightsholder, Jennifer Dunbar Dorn.

Ed Dorn, "Mesozoic Landscape" (broadside), produced by Holbrook Teter and Michael Myersl (Kent State Arts Festival, 1974).

Kenward Elmslie, "Ron Dossier" and "Hand," from *Tropicalism* (Z Press, 1975). Reprinted with permission of Ron Padgett as Trustee of the Kenward Gray Elmslie Revocable Trust.

Kenward Elmslie, selections, from *Cyberspace* (Granary Books, 2000). Reprinted with permission of Ron Padgett as Trustee of the Kenward Gray Elmslie Revocable Trust.

Kenward Elmslie, "Sin in the Hinterlands," reprinted from *Routine Disruptions* (Coffee House Press, 1998). © 1998 by Kenward Elmslie.

Baroness Elsa von Freytag-Loringhoven, from *Body Sweats, The Uncensored*

Writings of Elsa von Freytag-Loringhoven, edited by Irene Gammel and Suzanne Zelazo (MIT Press, 2011). © 2011 by the Massachusetts Institute of Technology.

Abraham Lincoln Gillespie, "A Poem From Puzlit," from *The Syntactic Revolution*, edited by Richard Milazzo (Out of London Press, 1980).

Michael Gottlieb, "Timing Is Everything," *This* magazine, edited by Barrett Watten. Reprinted with permission of the author.

Richard Huelsenbeck, "End of the World," from *The Dada Painters and Poets: An Anthology*, edited by Robert Motherwell, translated by Ralph Manheim (The Belknap Press of Harvard University Press, 1979).

Kenneth Koch, "Everyone is Endymion," "Gypsy Yo-yo," and "No Job at Sarah Lawrence," from *The Collected Poems of Kenneth Koch* (Knopf, 2005). © 2005 by the Kenneth Koch Literary Estate. Used by permission of Alfred A. Knopf, an imprint of Knopf Doubleday.

Mina Loy, "Crab-Angel," from "Songs to Joannes." Courtesy of Roger L. Conover, Estate of Mina Loy.

Jackson Mac Low, "Asymmetry 372," "Asymmetry 497," "2nd Light Poem: For Diane Wakoski—10 June 1962," "40TH DANCE—GIVING FALSELY—22 March 1964," and "A Lack of Balance But Not Fatal," from *Representative Works: 1938–1985* (Roof Books, 1986). Reprinted with permission of Anne Tardos.

Bernadette Mayer, "On Barnard," from *Ceremony Latin* (Angel Hair, 1975). Reprinted with permission of the author.

Bernadette Mayer, "François Villon Follows the Thin Lion," "Thick," and "We've Solved The Problem," from *Poetry and Early Poems* (Kulchur Foundation, 1976). Reprinted with permission of the author.

Bernadette Mayer, "A Catskill Eagle," from *Sonnets* (Tender Buttons, 1989). Reprinted with permission of the author.

Steve McCaffery, excerpt from "Teachable Texts," from *The Cheat of Words* (ECW press, 1996). Reproduced by permission of the author.

Taylor Mead, from *On Amphetamine and in Europe* (Boss Books, 1968). Reprinted with permission of the Taylor Mead Estate, Priscilla Mead.

Frank O'Hara, "Fantasy," from *Lunch Poems* (City Lights Books, 1964). © 1964 by Frank O'Hara. Reprinted with permission of The Permissions Company, LLC, on behalf of City Lights Books.

Peter Orlovsky, "Lines of Feeling," from *Clean Asshole Poems and Smiling Vegetable Songs* (City Lights Books, 1987). Reprinted with permission of the Estate of Peter A. Orlovsky.

Rochelle Owens, selections, from *Not Be Essence That Cannot Be* (Trobar, 1961). Reprinted with permission of the author.

Julie Patton, "word / A. just poem." Reprinted with permission of the author.

Bob Perelman, "PICTURE," "DON'T DRINK THE WATER, EAT THE FOOD, OR BREATHE THE AIR," "MENTAL IMAGERY," "UP MEMORY LANE," and "SCAPEGOAT," from *TEN to ONE* (Wesleyan University Press, 1999). Reprinted with permission of the author.

Francis Picabia, "Chimney Sperm," from *I am a Beautiful Monster*, translated by Marc Lowenthal (MIT Press, 2007). Reprinted with permission of MIT Press.

Bern Porter, "What's filling lake Michigan faster than waste? Algae.," from *Found Poems* (Nightboat Books, 2011).

Tom Raworth, from *Collected Poems* (Carcanet, 2003). © the estate of Tom Raworth. Reprinted with permission of Margaret Valarie Raworth.

Aram Saroyan, "oh oh oh oh oh oh oh oh," from *The Complete Minimalist Poems* (Ugly Duckling Presse, 2007). © 2007 by Aram Saroyan. Reprinted with permission of the author.

Sun Ra, "Nuclear War." © Enterplanetary Koncepts (BMI). Reprinted by permission of Sun Ra LLC and SunRa.com (Irwin Chusid, administrator).

Anne Tardos, selections from "Ginkgo Knuckle Nubia," from *The Dik-dik's Solitude: New & Selected Works* (Granary Books, 2003). Reprinted with permission of the author.

Tristan Tzara, from *Dada Manifestos*, translated by Ralph Manheim (Alma Books). Reprinted with permission of Alma Books.

Tristan Tzara, "Metal Coughdrops," translated by Jerome Rothenberg (Alma Books). Reprinted with permission of Alma Books.

Hannah Weiner, from *Weeks* (Xexoxial Editions, 1990). Reprinted with permission of Charles Bernstein for Hannah Weiner in trust.

William Carlos Williams, "Breakfast" and "The Hermaphroditic Telephones," from *The Collected Poems: Volume I, 1909–1939* (New Directions Publishing

Corp, 1938). Reprinted by permission of New Directions Publishing Corp. UK William Carlos Williams permissions © Carcanet.

William Carlos Williams, "Hey Red!," from *The Collected Poems: Volume II, 1939–1962* (New Directions Publishing Corp, 1946). Reprinted by permission of New Directions Publishing Corp. UK William Carlos Williams permissions © Carcanet.

All possible care has been taken to trace ownership and secure permission for the work quoted in this book. If any required acknowledgments have been omitted, it is unintentional.

www.ingramcontent.com/pod-product-compliance
Lightning Source LLC
Chambersburg PA
CBHW020924230426
43666CB00008B/1557